Road Atlas of

Norfolk County

Massachusetts

Data Sources:

U.S. Census Bureau

U.S. Fish & Wildlife Service

U.S. Geological Survey

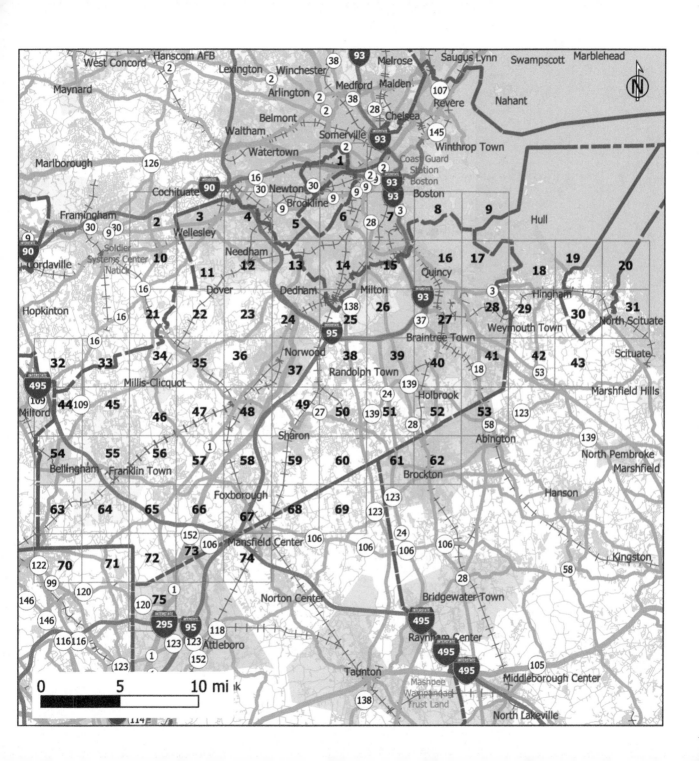

LEGEND

⌐⌐	County Boundary	📷	Cliff
☐	Township Boundary	⪢	Dam/Levee
☐	Municipal Boundary	💧	Falls
▨	Water	⚓	Harbor
▨	Military Installation	🚁	Heliport
▨	Native American Area	✚	Hospital
▨	Park	Π	Mine
▬▬	Interstate Highway	🌳	Park
▬▬	US Route	✉	Post Office
▬▬	State Route	🏫	School
—	Local Road	♨	Spring
⊢⊢⊢	Railway	▲	Summit
✈	Airport	📡	Tower
⚱	Cemetery	❋	Well
✝	Church		

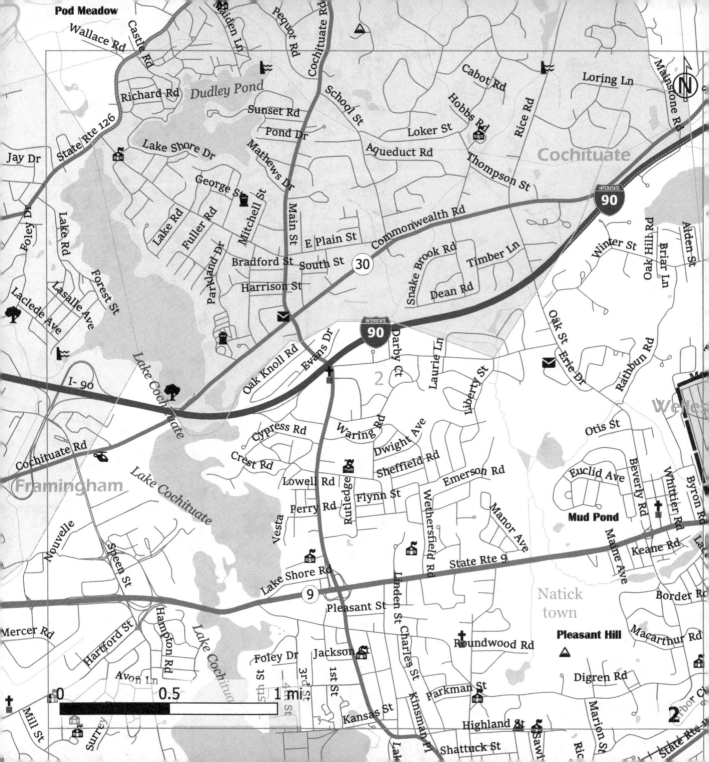

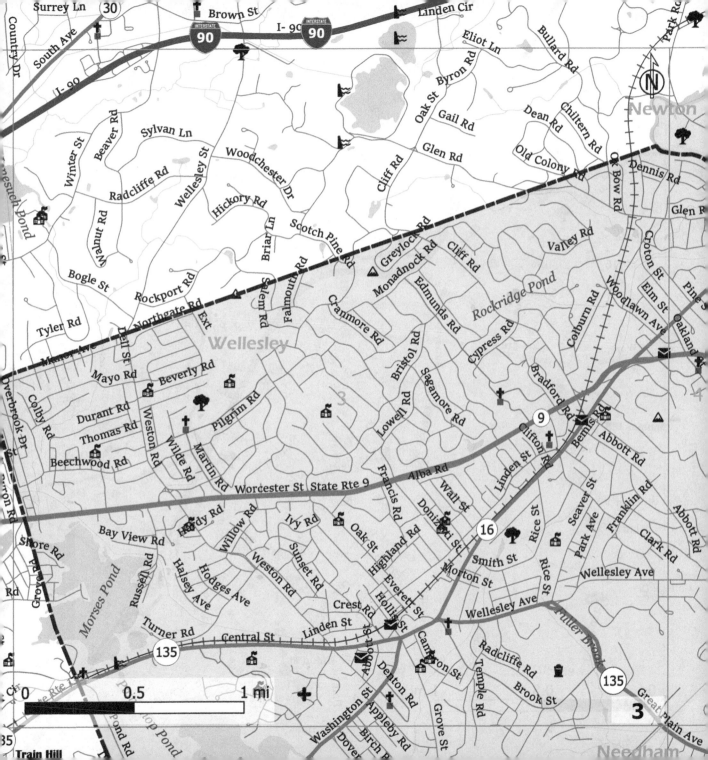

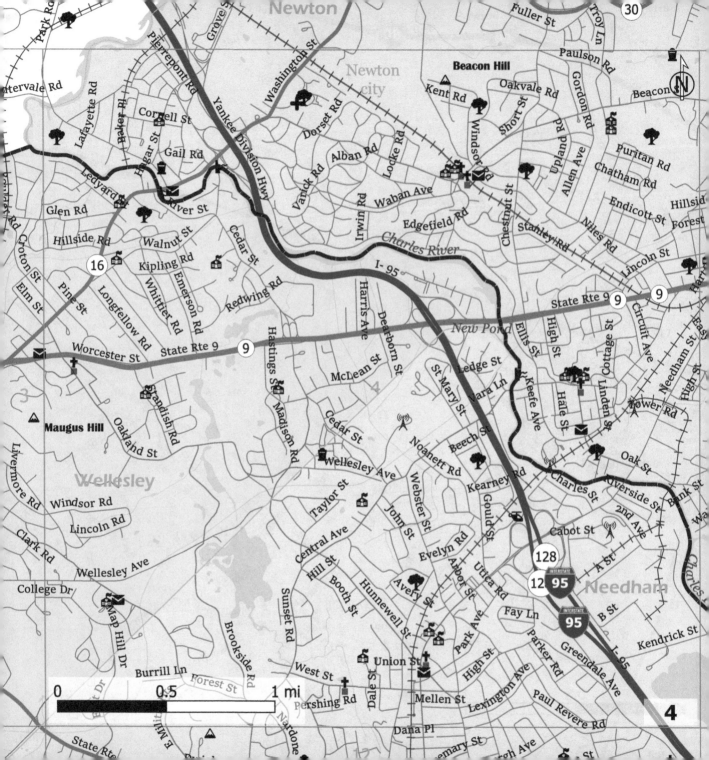

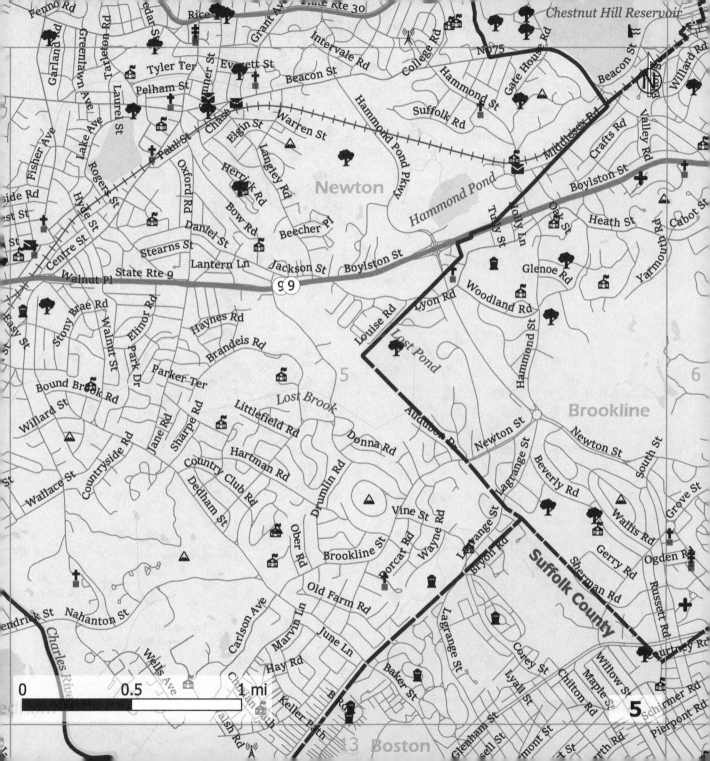

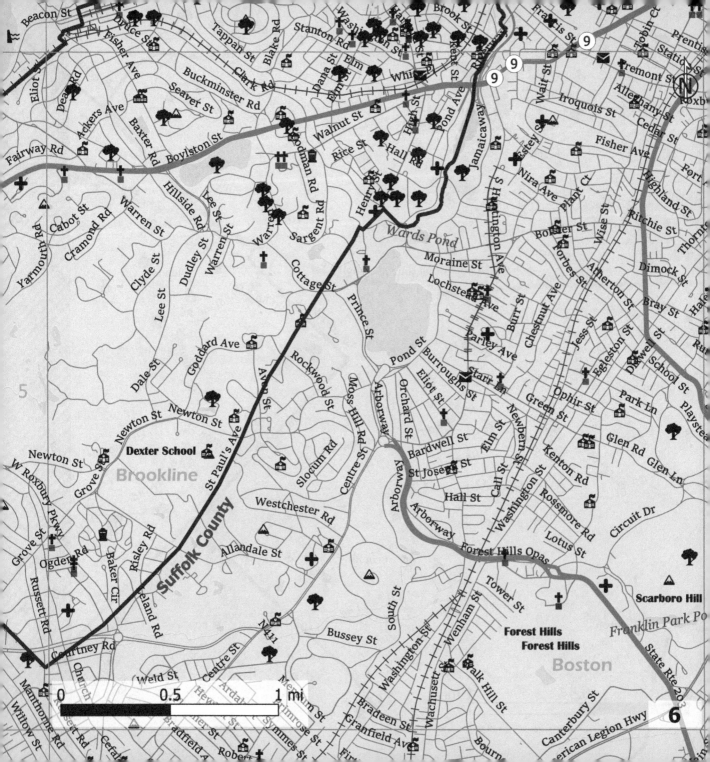

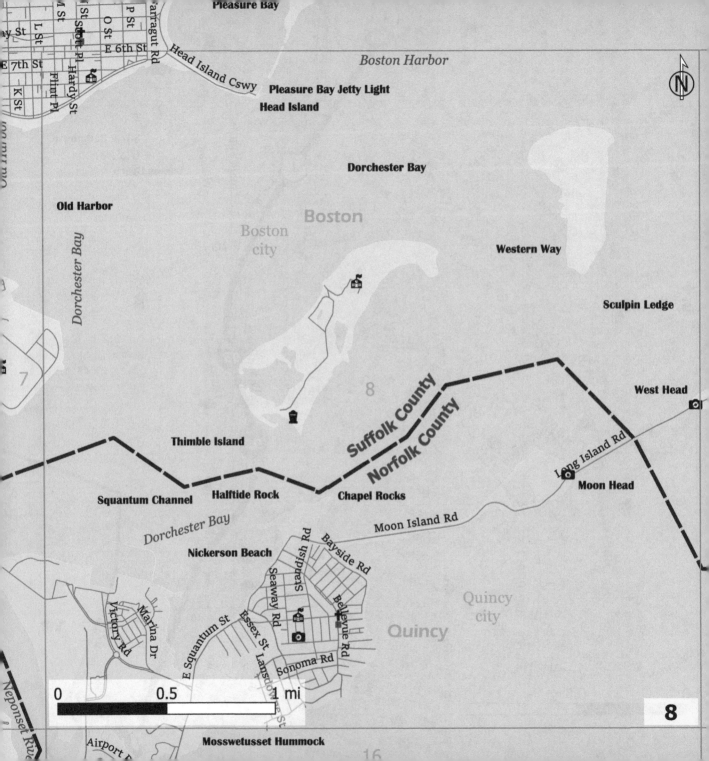

Pleasure Bay

St St

P St

O St E 6th St

Head Island Cswy

Boston Harbor

7th St

E

Hardy St

Farragut Rd

Pleasure Bay Jetty Light

Head Island

K St

Flint Pl

Dorchester Bay

Old Harbor

Boston

Boston
city

Western Way

Dorchester Bay

Sculpin Ledge

8

Suffolk County

West Head

Thimble Island

Norfolk County

Long Island Rd

Squantum Channel

Halftide Rock

Chapel Rocks

Moon Head

Dorchester Bay

Moon Island Rd

Nickerson Beach

Standish Rd

Bayside Rd

Quincy
city

Seaway Rd

Victory Rd

Marina Dr

E Squantum St

Essex St

Bellevue Rd

Quincy

Sonoma Rd

Lansdowne St

0   0.5   1 mi

8

Neponset River

Airport

Mosswetusset Hummock

16

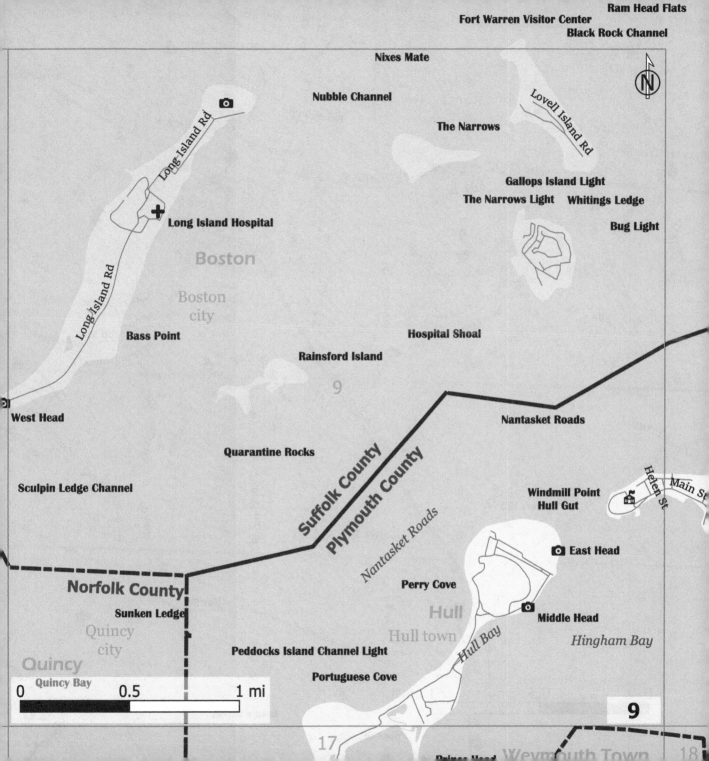

Ram Head Flats

Fort Warren Visitor Center

Black Rock Channel

Nixes Mate

Nubble Channel

Lovell Island Rd

The Narrows

Long Island Rd

Gallops Island Light

The Narrows Light   Whitings Ledge

Long Island Hospital

Bug Light

Boston

Boston
city

Long Island Rd

Bass Point

Hospital Shoal

Rainsford Island

9

West Head

Nantasket Roads

Quarantine Rocks

Suffolk County

Plymouth County

Sculpin Ledge Channel

Nantasket Roads

Windmill Point
Hull Gut

Helen St

Main St

East Head

Norfolk County

Perry Cove

Middle Head

Sunken Ledge

Hull

Hingham Bay

Quincy
city

Hull town

Quincy

Hull Bay

Peddocks Island Channel Light

Quincy Bay

Portuguese Cove

0   0.5   1 mi

9

17

Prince Head   Weymouth Town   18

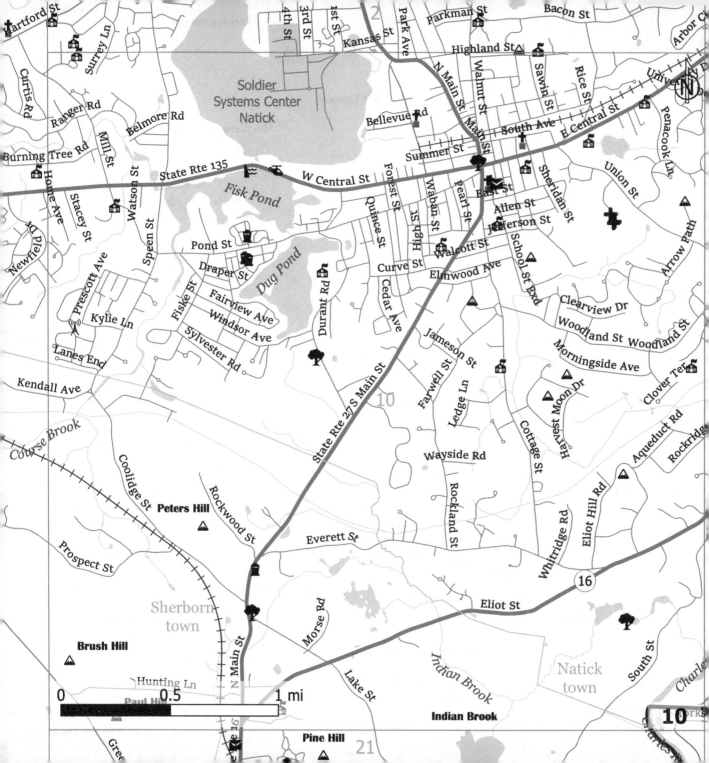

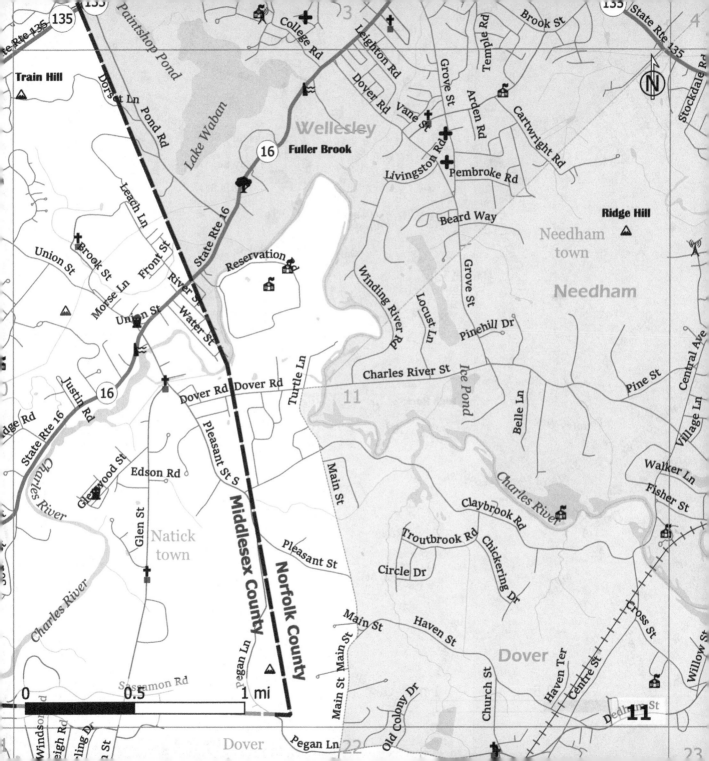

State Rte 135

135

135

State Rte 135

4

3

Brook St

Temple Rd

College Rd

Leighton Rd

Grove St

Dover Rd

Vane St

Arden Rd

Cartwright Rd

Stockdale Rd

N

Train Hill

Paintshop Pond

Dorset Ln

Pond Rd

Lake Waban

Wellesley

16

Fuller Brook

Livingston Rd

Pembroke Rd

Beard Way

Ridge Hill

Needham town

Needham

Leach Ln

Union St

Brook St

Front St

State Rte 16

River St

Reservation Rd

Winding River Rd

Locust Ln

Grove St

Pinehill Dr

Morse Ln

Union St

Water St

Charles River St

Ice Pond

Belle Ln

Pine St

Central Ave

Village Ln

Justin Rd

16

Dover Rd   Dover Rd

Turtle Ln

11

Walker Ln

Fisher St

ge Rd

State Rte 16

Charles River

Glenwood St

Edson Rd

Pleasant St S

Main St

Charles River

Claybrook Rd

Glen St

Natick town

Middlesex County

Norfolk County

Pleasant St

Troutbrook Rd

Chickering Dr

Circle Dr

Main St

Main St

Haven St

Cross St

Main St

Old Colony Dr

Church St

Haven Ter

Centre St

Dover

Willow St

11

Windsor

d

Pegan Ln

Sassamon Rd

1 mi

0   0.5

ring Dr

n St

eigh Rd

Dover

Pegan Ln

22

Dedham St

23

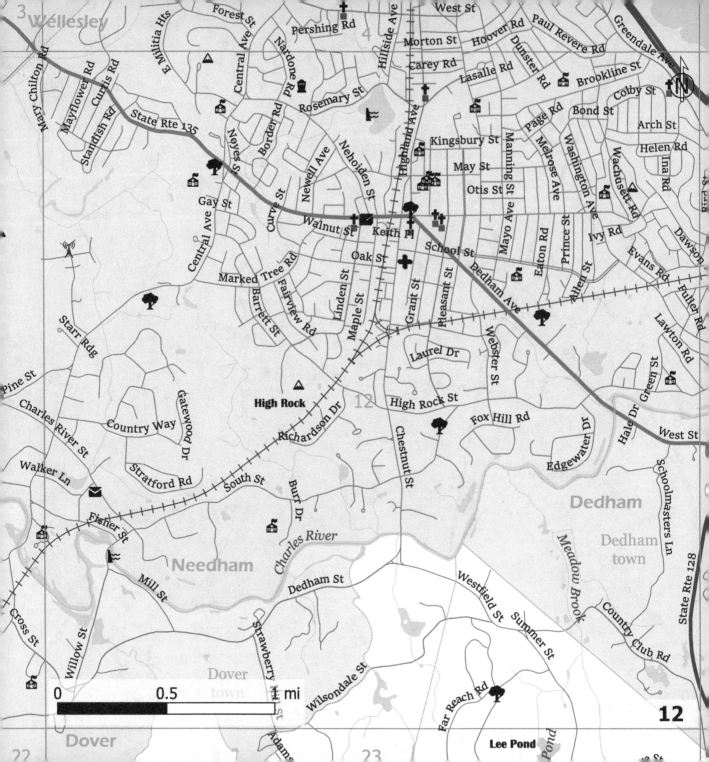

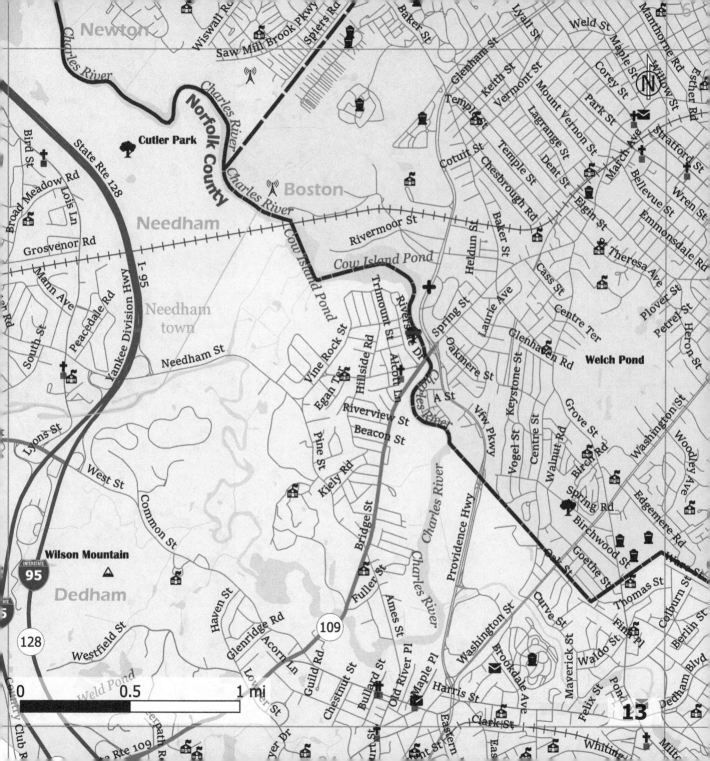

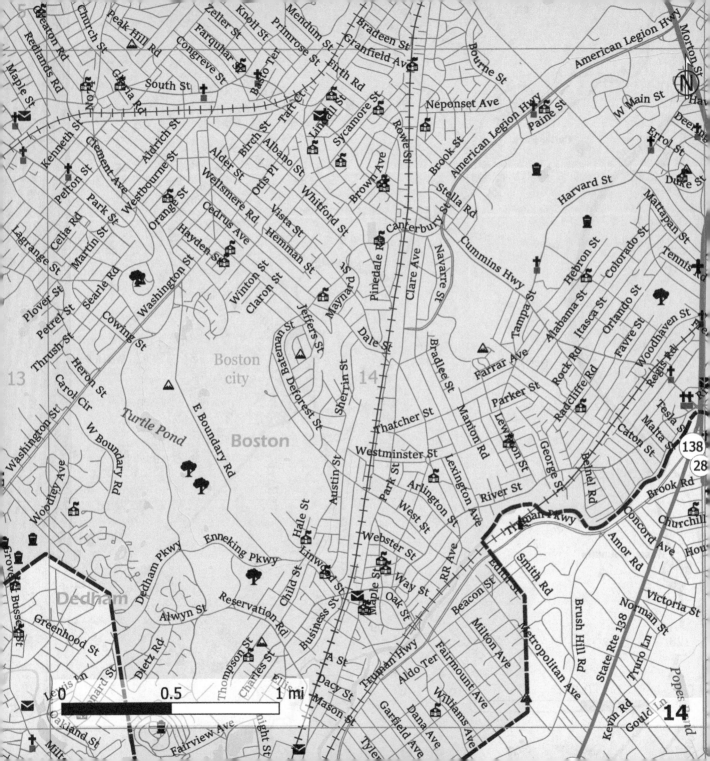

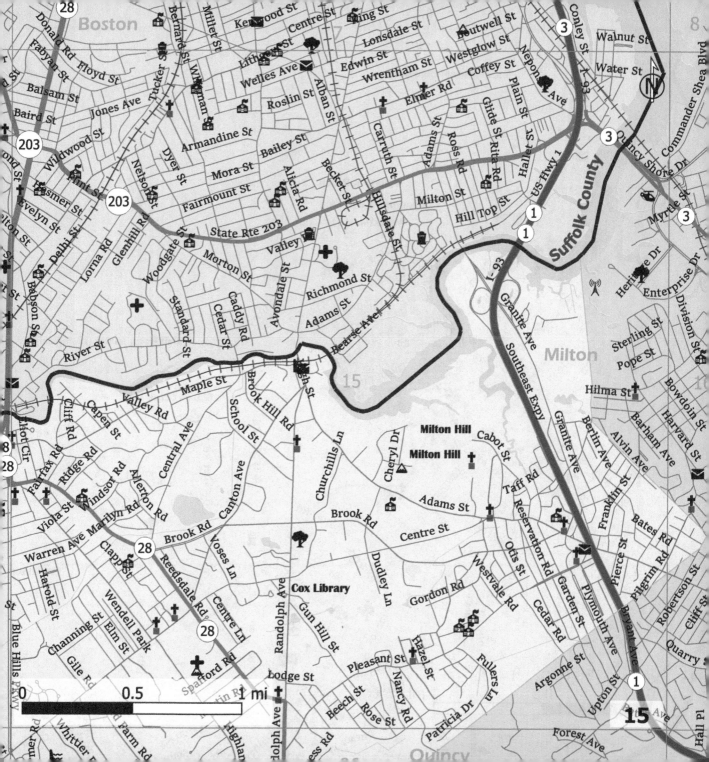

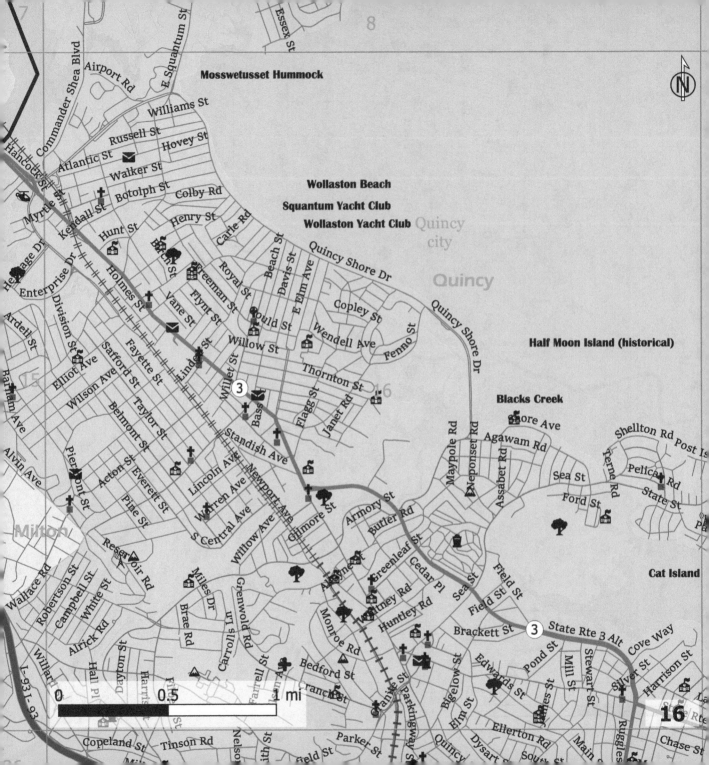

Mosswetusset Hummock

Wollaston Beach

Squantum Yacht Club

Wollaston Yacht Club

Quincy city

Quincy

Half Moon Island (historical)

Blacks Creek

Cat Island

Commander Shea Blvd
Airport Rd
Williams St
Russell St
Hovey St
Atlantic St
Walker St
Botolph St
Colby Rd
Henry St
Carle Rd
Hunt St
Beach St
Davis St
Quincy Shore Dr
E Elm Ave
Copley St
Fenmo St
Quincy Shore Dr
Shore Ave
Royal St
Gould St
Wendell Ave
Willow St
Thornton St
Janet Rd
Agawam Rd
Sea St
Shellton Rd Post Is
Maypole Rd
Neponset Rd
Assabet Rd
Ford St
Terne Rd
Pelican Rd
State St
Standish Ave
Bass St
Flagg St
Armory St
Butler Rd
Greenleaf St
Cedar Pl
Sea St
Field St
Field St
Lincoln Ave
Newport Ave
Gilmore St
Whitney Rd
Huntley Rd
Brackett St
Pond St
Mill St
Stewart St
Silver St
Cove Way
Harrison St
Monroe Rd
Bedford St
Cranch St
Bigelow St
Edwards St
James St
Ruggles St
State Rte 3 Alt
Ellerton Rd
Parker St
Quincy
Dysart St

Heritage Dr
Hancock St
Myrtle St
Kendall St
Enterprise Dr
Division St
Holmes St
Birch St
Freeman St
Royal St
Vane St
Flynt St
Linden St
Fayette St
Willet St
Ardell St
Elliot Ave
Safford St
Wilson Ave
Belmont St
Taylor St
Acton St
Everett St
Pine St
Pierpont St
S Everett St
Reservoir Rd
Warren Ave
S Central Ave
Willow Ave
Miles Dr
Brae Rd
Grenwold Rd
Carroll Dr
Alvin Ave
Barham Ave
Wallace Rd
Robertson St
Campbell St
White St
Alrick Rd
Dayton St
Hall Pl
Willard
L-93 L-93
Copeland St
Tinson Rd
Nelson
Farrell St
Bedford St
Granite St
Parkingway St
Elm St
Pond St
South St
Main St
Chase St

0   0.5   1 mi

N

8

7

15

16

16

16

Milton

3

3

Quincy Bay

Hangman Island

9

Hingham Bay

Hull

Prince Head

Hull Bay

Wreck Rock

Nantasket Roads

Hull town

Plymouth County

N

West Gut

Pig Rock Light

Norfolk County

Sheep Island

Hull Bay

Nut Island

Houghs Neck

Weymouth Fore River
Hingham Bay

Quincy
city

Veazie Rocks

Seal Rock

Weymouth
Town city

Island Ave

Quincy

Quincy Yacht Club
Spiers Stand

17

Winthrop St

Manet Ave

Wall St

Weymouth Town

Stoughton St

Babcock St

Charles St

Manet Beach

Weymouth Fore River

18

Sea St

Darrow St

Marine St

Raccoon Island

Lower Neck Cove

Jewett St

Rhoda St

Hooper St

8th Ave

Hood St

William K Webb Park

Mead St

Rock Island Cove

Rock Island Head

Chesley Rd

Broady Ave

Grace Rd

Doane St

Gull Point

Bass Rock

Fort Point

Rose Cliff

Upper Neck

Bowes Ave

Jacknife Ledge

Eastern Neck

Parnell St

River St

Hole Point

Philip Head

Bicknell St

Weymouth Back River

Regatta Rd

North St

Neck St

Fogg Way

Lincoln St

Shipyard Point

Squanto Rd

Pilgrim Rd

Beal St

17

0   0.5   1 mi

3

State Rte 3 Alt

28

Babcock Ave

Sea St

State Rte 3 Alt

3

Bare Cove

Fottler St

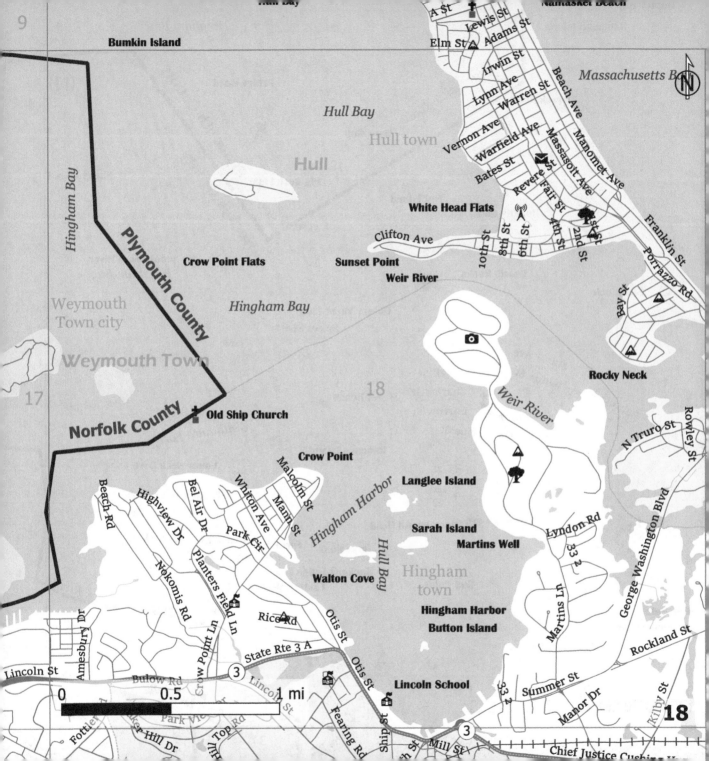

Bumkin Island

Hull Bay

Hull town

Hull

Massachusetts Bay

A St
Lewis St
Elm St   Adams St
Irwin St
Lynn Ave
Warren St
Vernon Ave
Beach Ave
Manomet Ave
Warfield Ave
Massasoit Ave
Bates St
White Head Flats
Revere St
Fair St
4th St
2nd St
Franklin St
Porrazzo Rd

Hingham Bay

Clifton Ave
Sunset Point
Weir River
10th St
8th St
6th St

Crow Point Flats

Weymouth
Town city

Plymouth County

Weymouth Town

17

18

Weir River

📷

Rocky Neck

Bay St

Norfolk County

✝ Old Ship Church

N Truro St
Rowley St

Crow Point

Malcolm St

Langlee Island

Weir River

Bel Air Dr
Whiton Ave
Mann St

Hingham Harbor

Sarah Island
Martins Well

Lyndon Rd
33

Highview Dr
Park Cir

Hull Bay

Martins Ln
33

George Washington Blvd

Beach Rd

Nokomis Rd
Planters Field Ln

Walton Cove

Hingham
town

Hingham Harbor
Button Island

Rice Rd

Otis St

Rockland St

Amesbury Dr

State Rte 3 A
Lincoln St
Bulow Rd

(3)

Lincoln St

1 mi

Otis St

Lincoln School

33

Summer St

Manor Dr

Kilby St

18

0   0.5   1 mi

Park View

Fottler

ker Hill Dr

Top Rd

Fearing Rd

Ship

Mill St

(3)

Chief Justice Cushing H

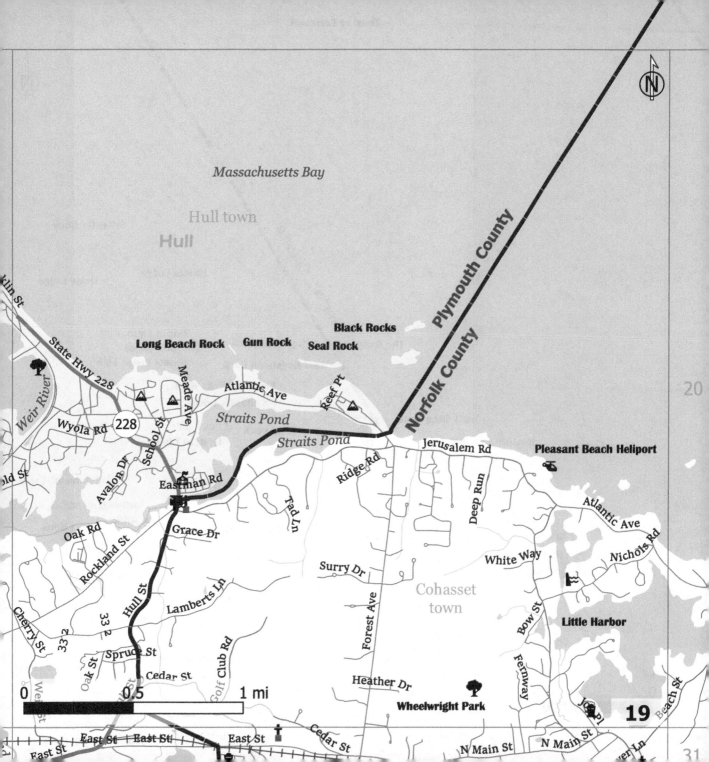

Massachusetts Bay

Hull town

Hull

Black Rocks

Long Beach Rock   Gun Rock   Seal Rock

Plymouth County

Norfolk County

N

Franklin St

State Hwy 228

Weir River

Wyola Rd   228

Old St

Avalon Dr

School St

Meade Ave

Atlantic Ave

Reef Pt

Straits Pond

Straits Pond

Jerusalem Rd

Ridge Rd

Deep Run

Pleasant Beach Heliport

Eastman Rd

Grace Dr

Tad Ln

Surry Dr

Atlantic Ave

Nichols Rd

White Way

20

Oak Rd

Rockland St

Lamberts Ln

Forest Ave

Cohasset town

Bow St

Little Harbor

Cherry St

33

33

Hull St

Oak St

Spruce St

Cedar St

Golf Club Rd

Heather Dr

Wheelwright Park

Fernway

Joe Pl

Beach St

19

0   0.5   1 mi

Weir

East St   East St   East St

Cedar St

N Main St   N Main St

31

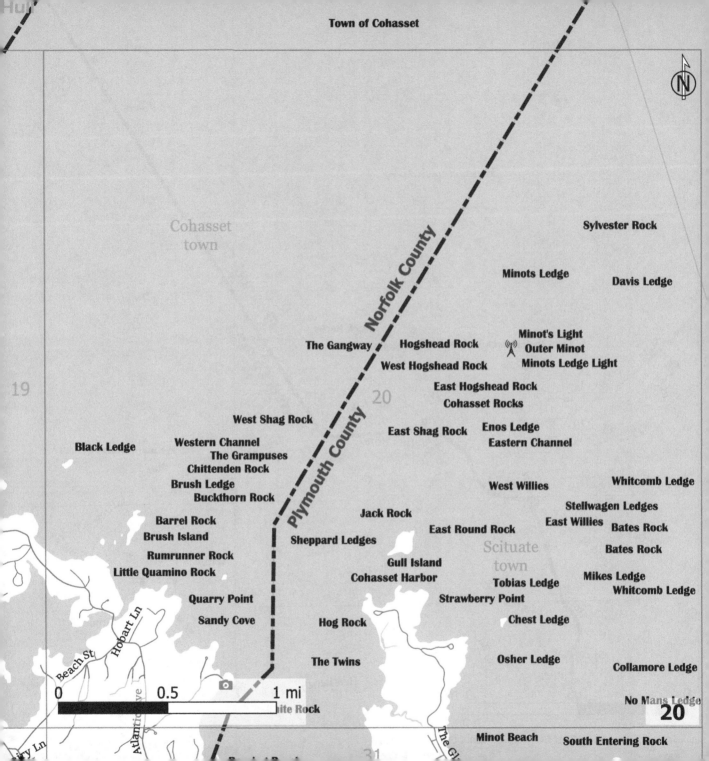

N

Sylvester Rock

Cohasset town

Minots Ledge

Davis Ledge

Norfolk County

The Gangway   Hogshead Rock   Minot's Light
                                             Outer Minot
                West Hogshead Rock   Minots Ledge Light

                                   East Hogshead Rock
                                   Cohasset Rocks

Plymouth County   20

West Shag Rock   East Shag Rock   Enos Ledge
                                                     Eastern Channel

Black Ledge

Western Channel
        The Grampuses
    Chittenden Rock   West Willies   Whitcomb Ledge

Brush Ledge   Stellwagen Ledges
    Buckthorn Rock   East Willies   Bates Rock

                           Jack Rock
Barrel Rock   East Round Rock   Bates Rock
Brush Island   Sheppard Ledges
                                                     Scituate
Rumrunner Rock   town
Little Quamino Rock   Gull Island   Mikes Ledge
                                  Cohasset Harbor   Tobias Ledge   Whitcomb Ledge

Quarry Point   Strawberry Point

Sandy Cove   Chest Ledge

                           Hog Rock

Beach St   Hobart Ln   Osher Ledge
                                                                      Collamore Ledge
              The Twins

0   0.5   1 mi
                                                                      No Mans Ledge

                                                                      20

White Rock

Minot Beach   South Entering Rock

19

Hull

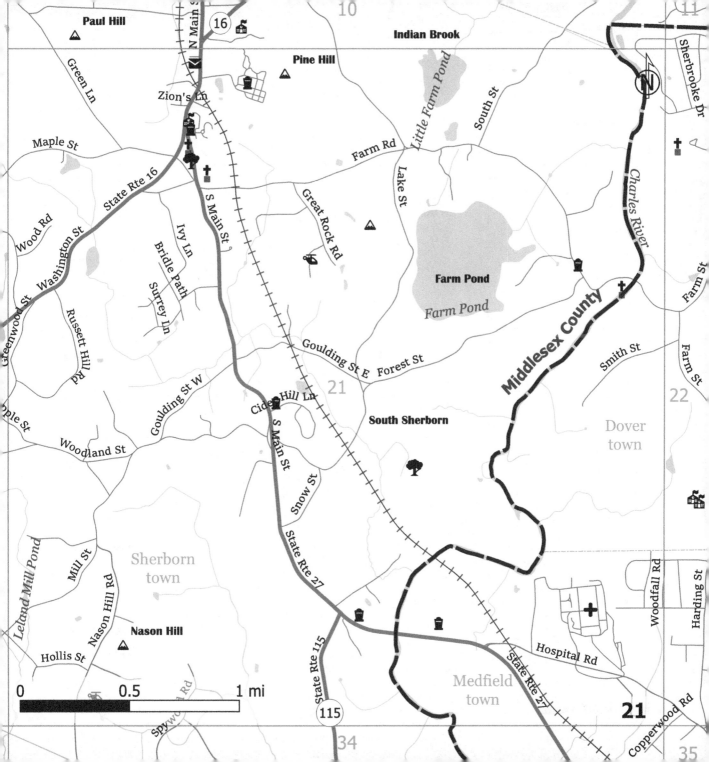

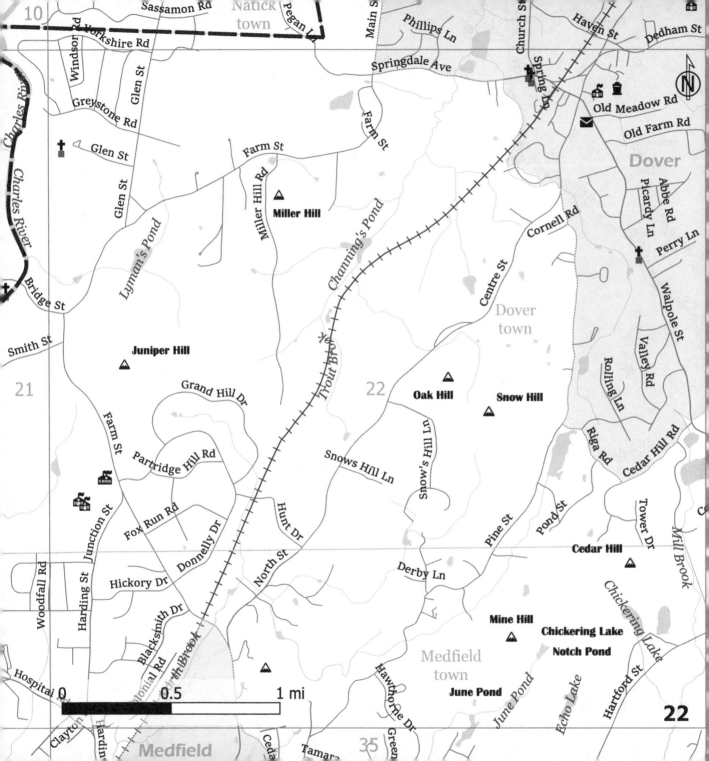

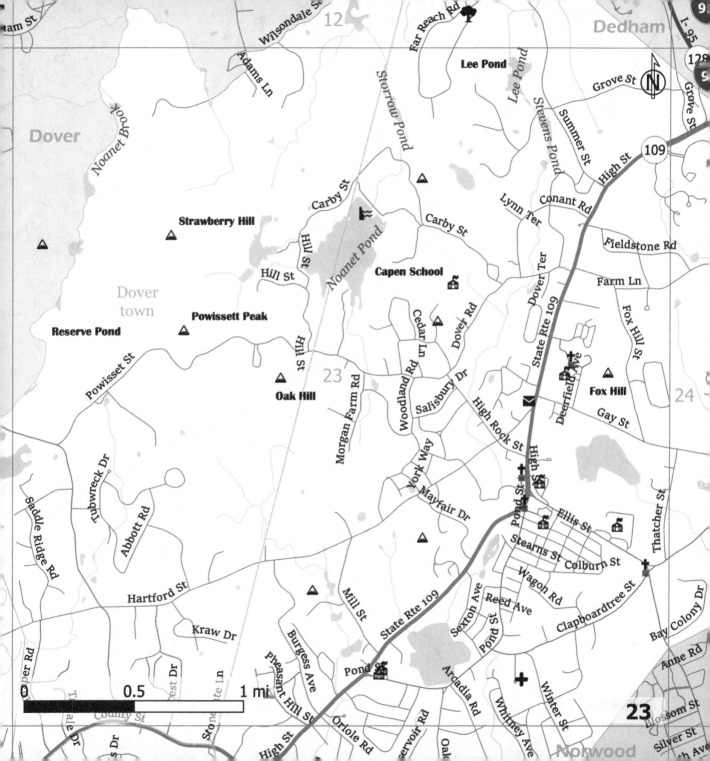

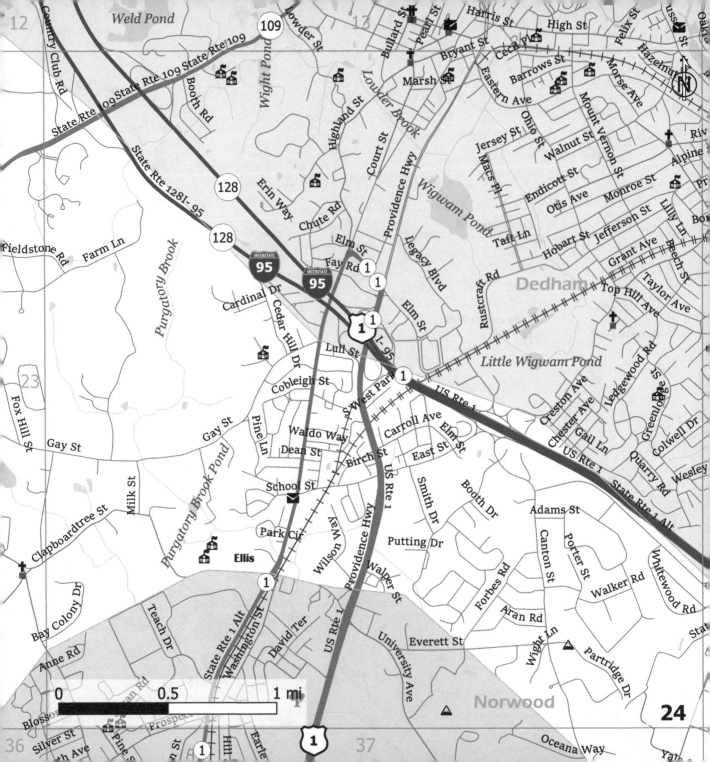

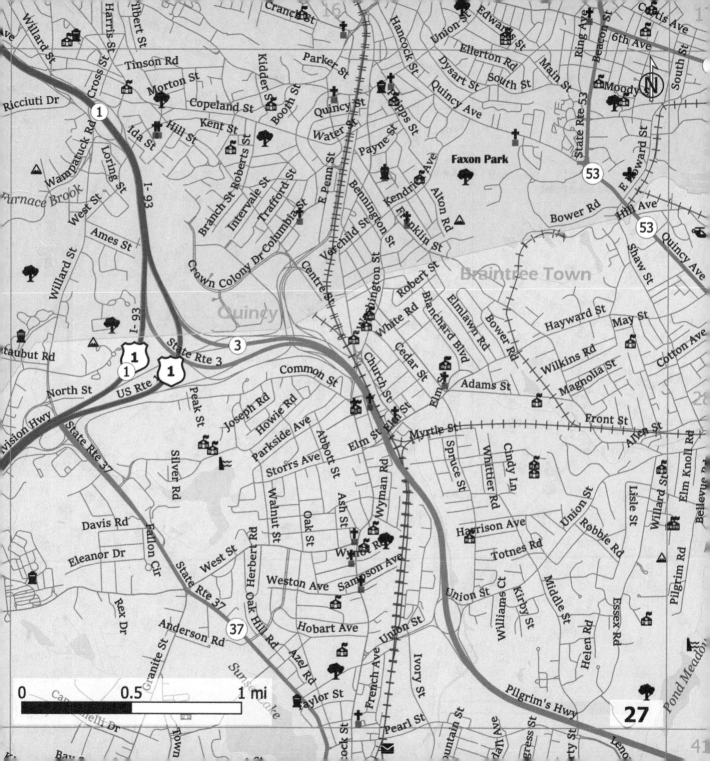

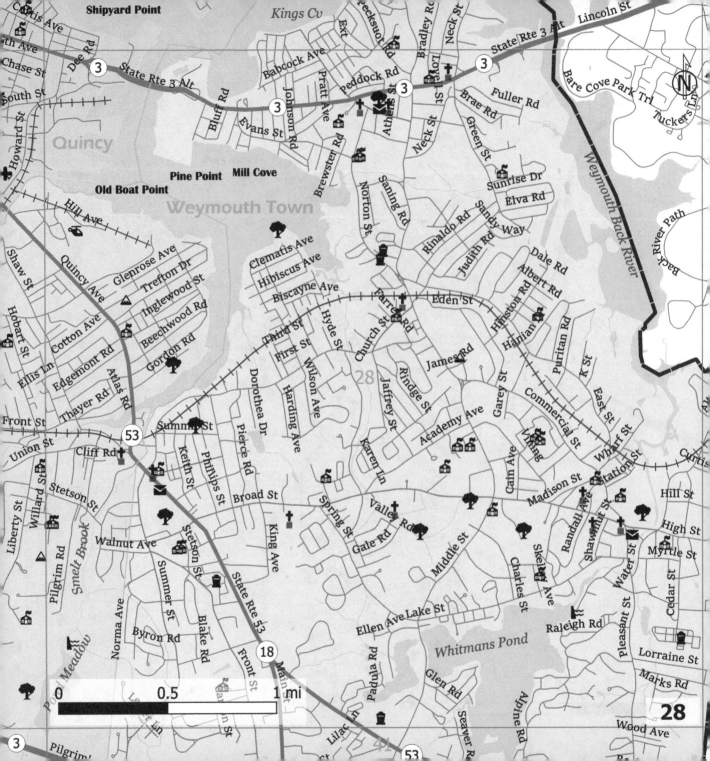

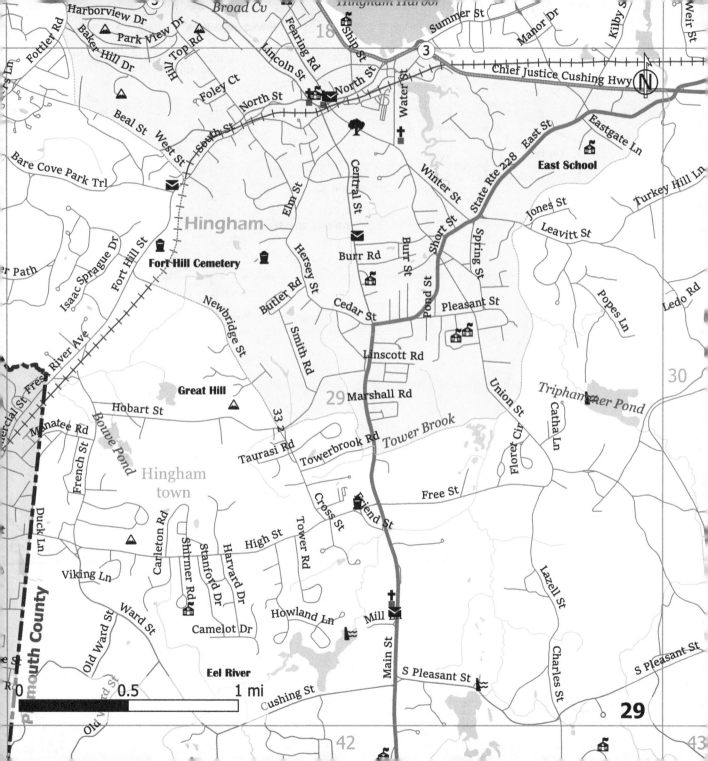

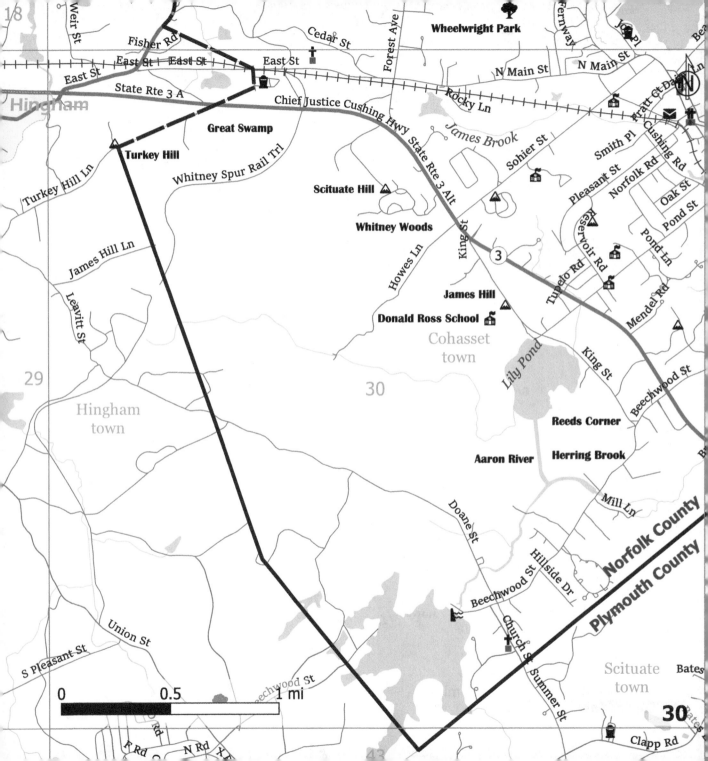

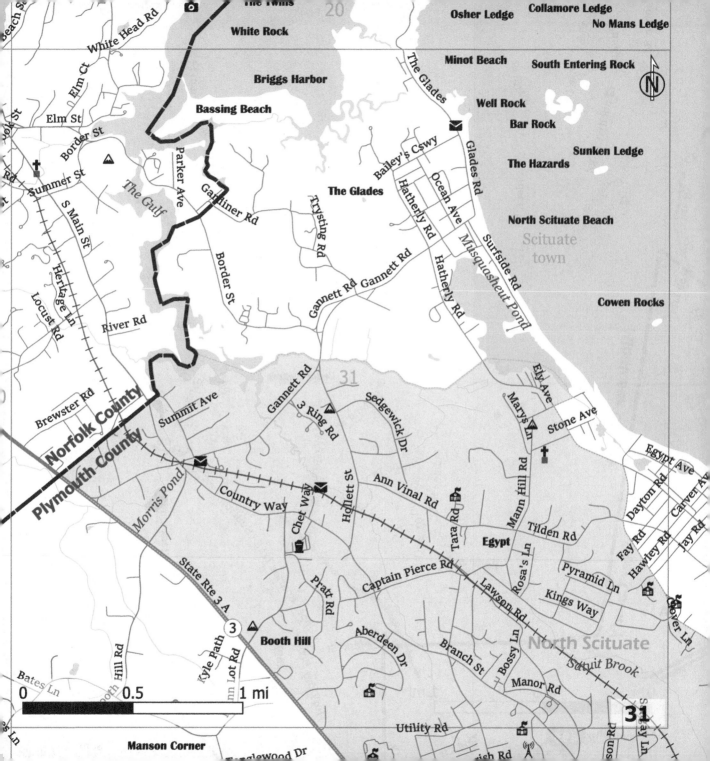

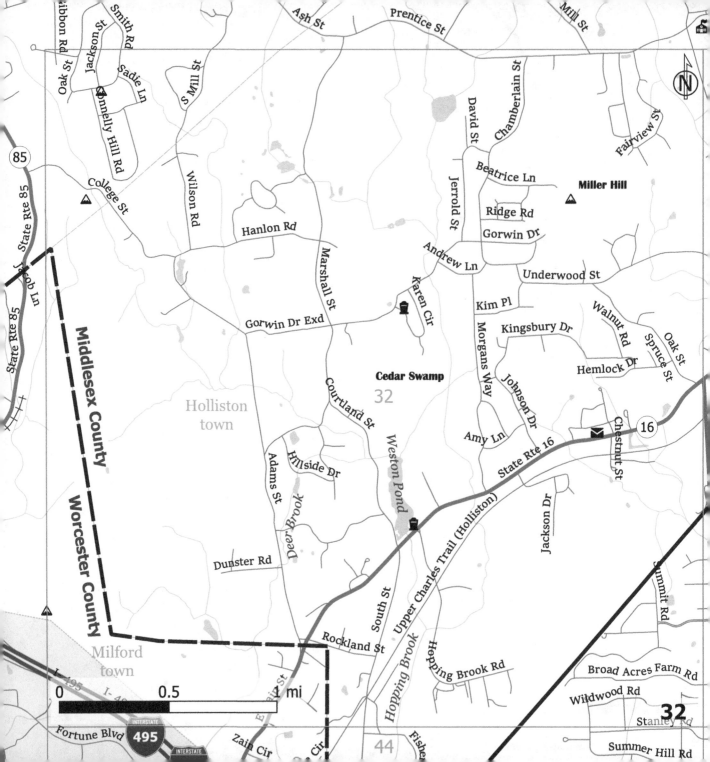

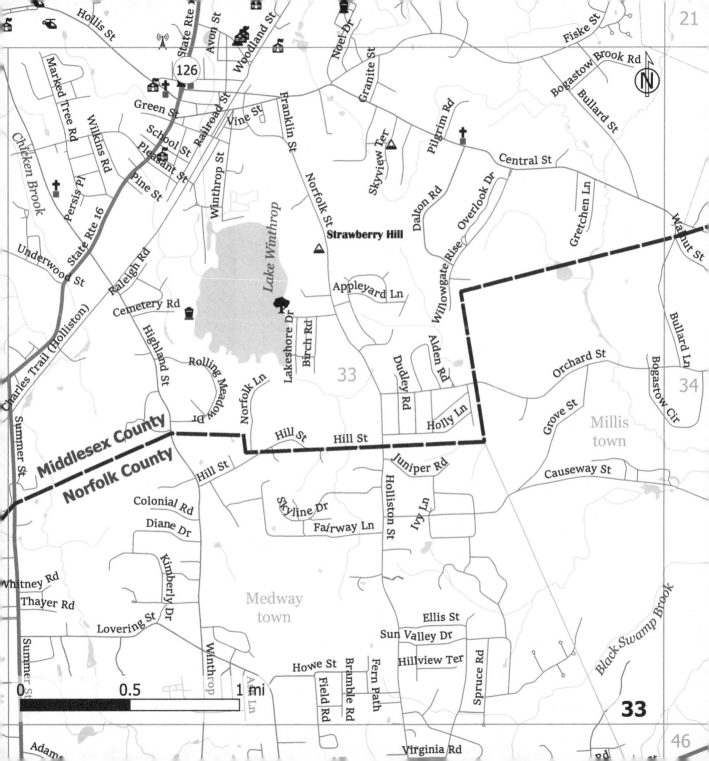

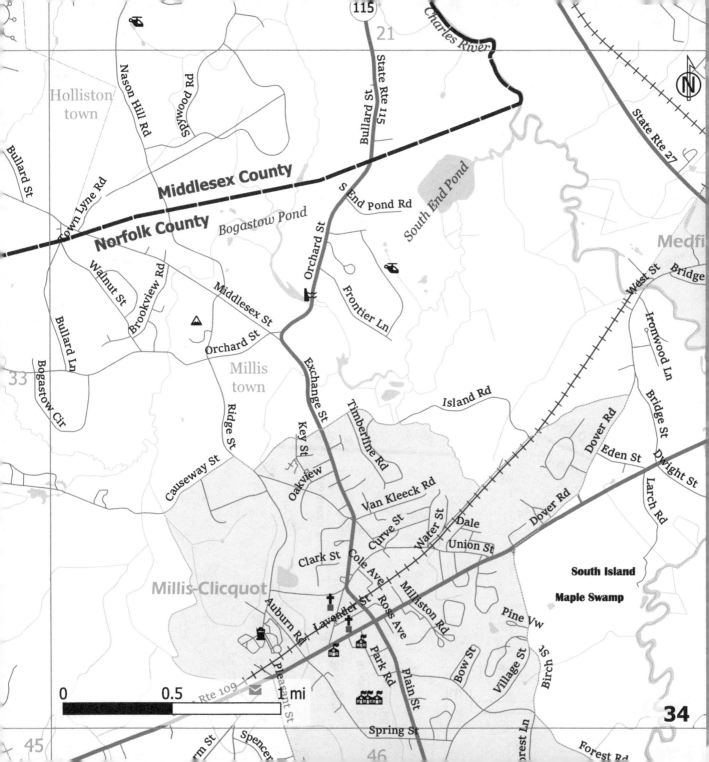

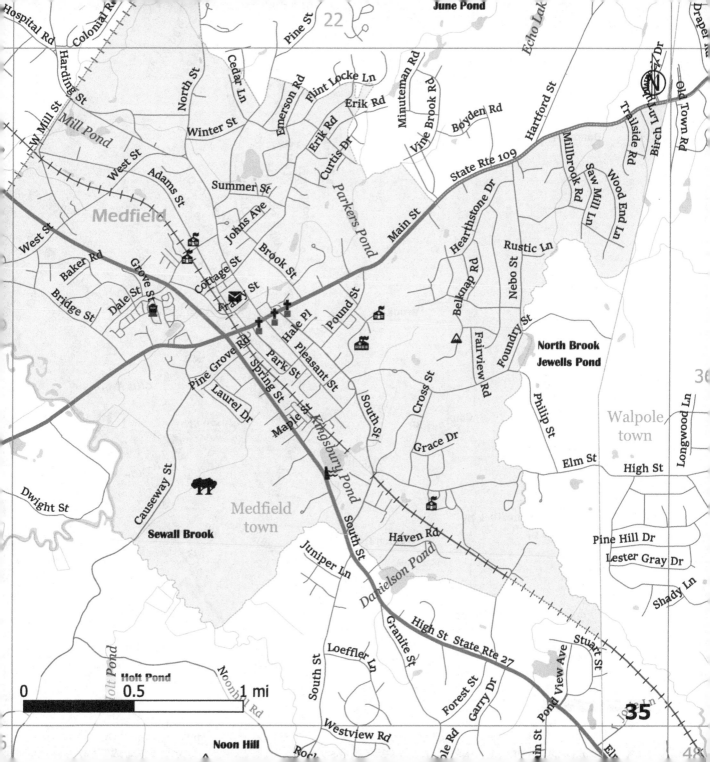

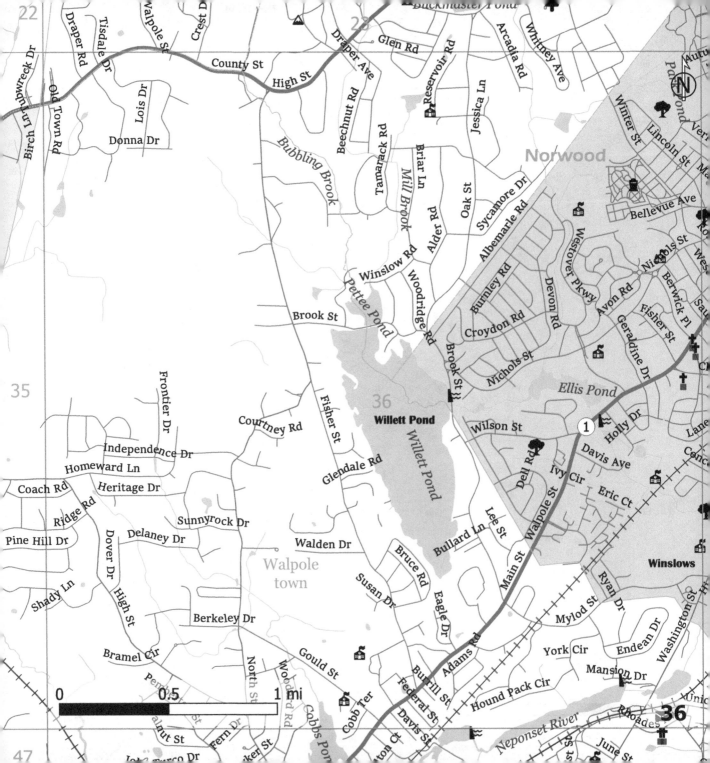

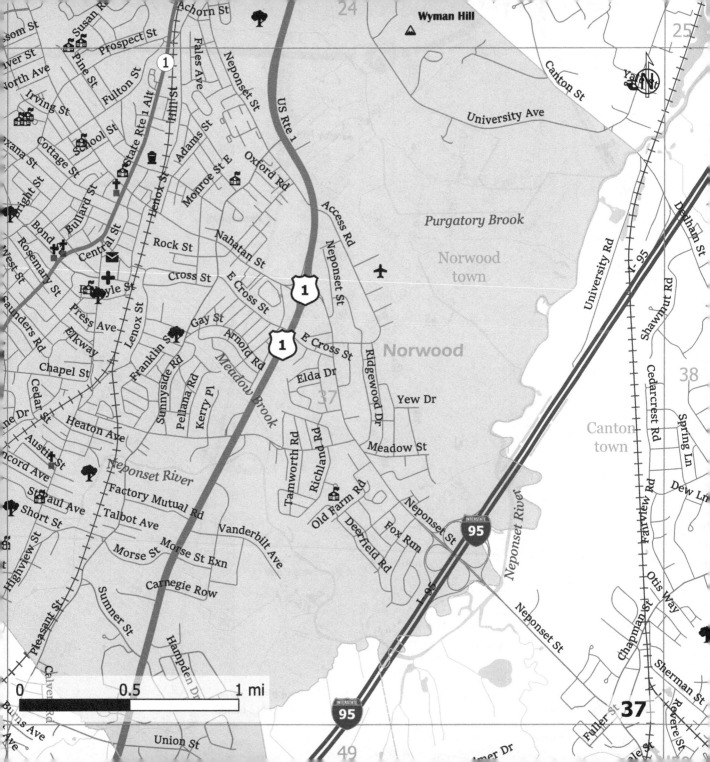

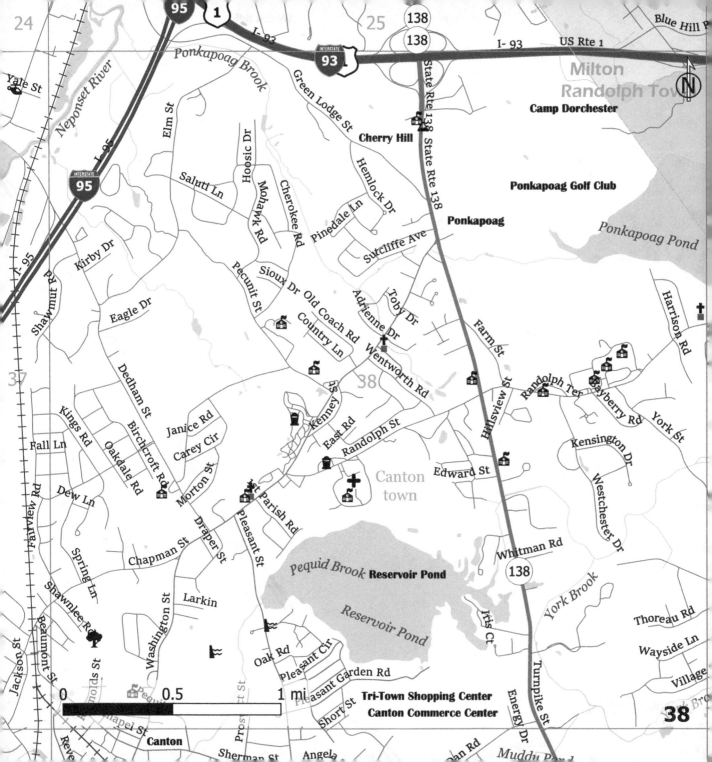

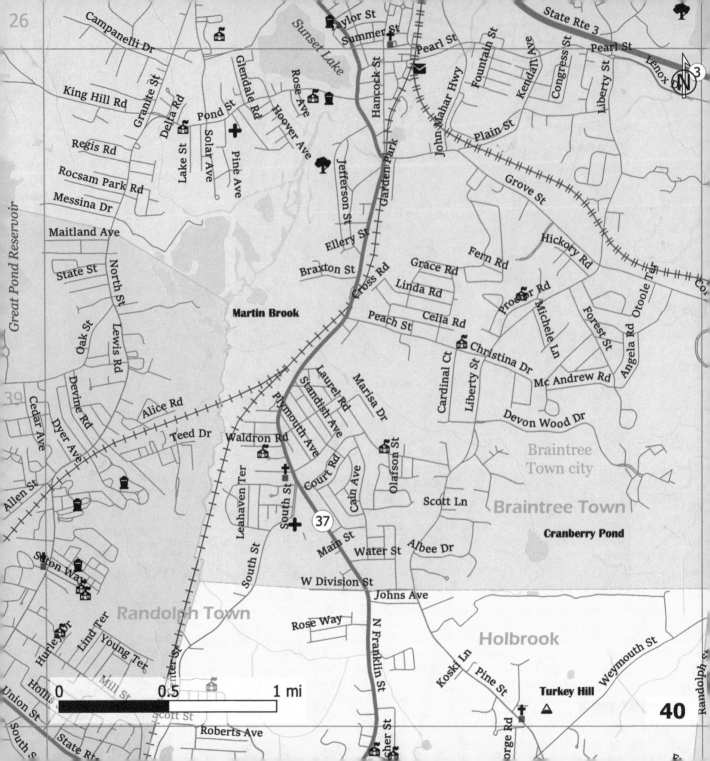

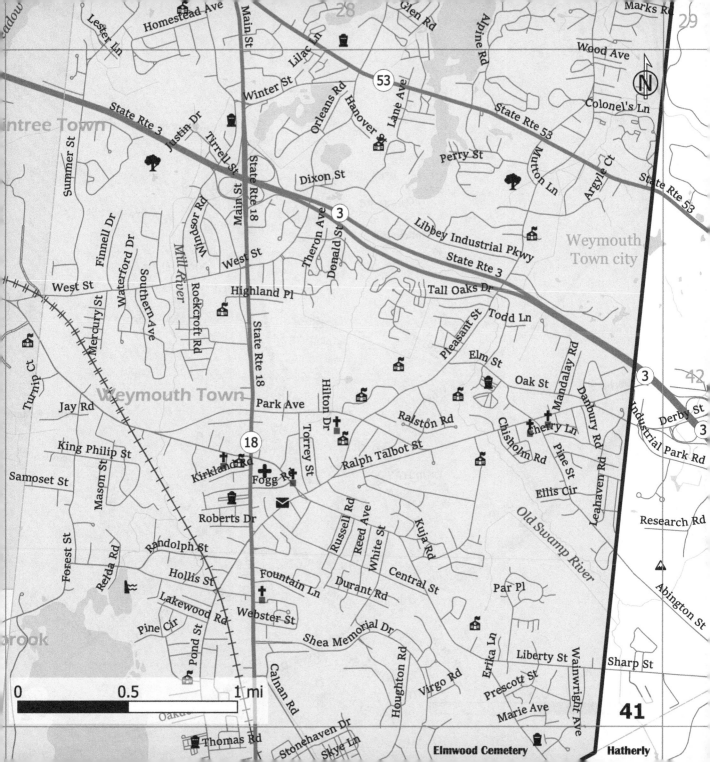

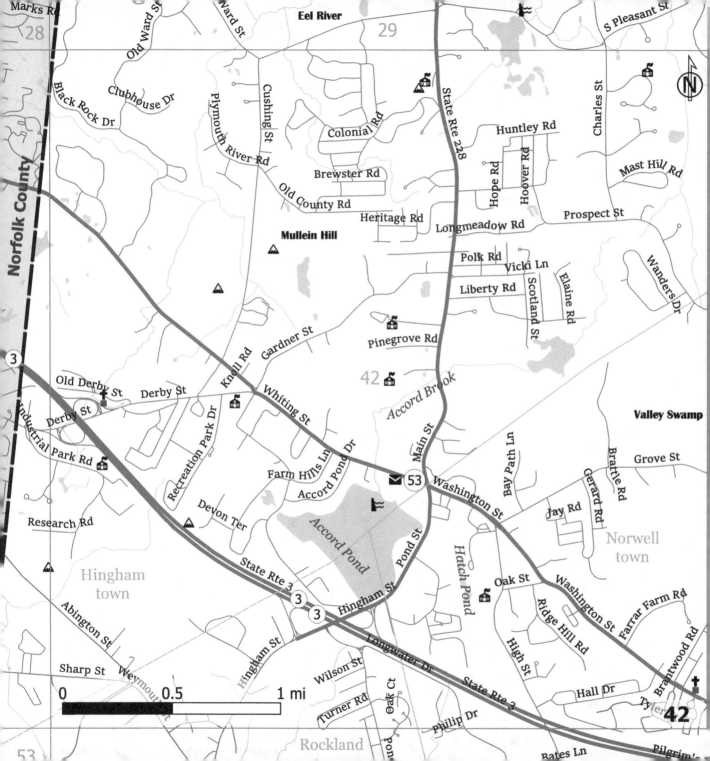

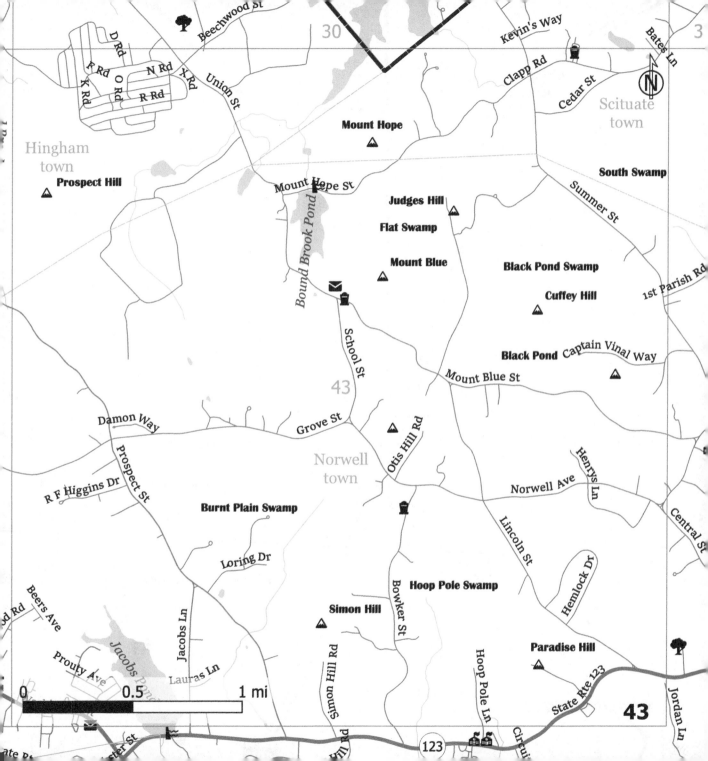

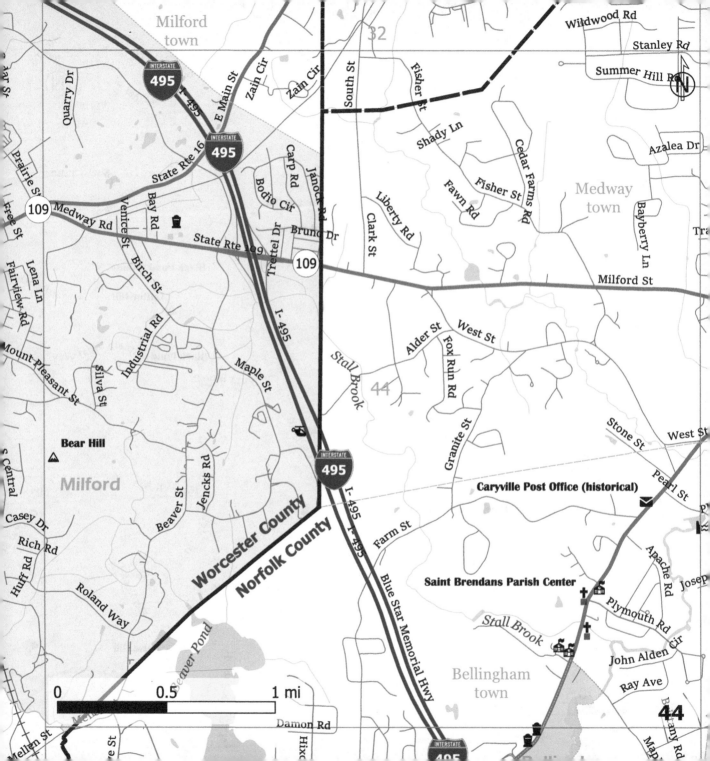

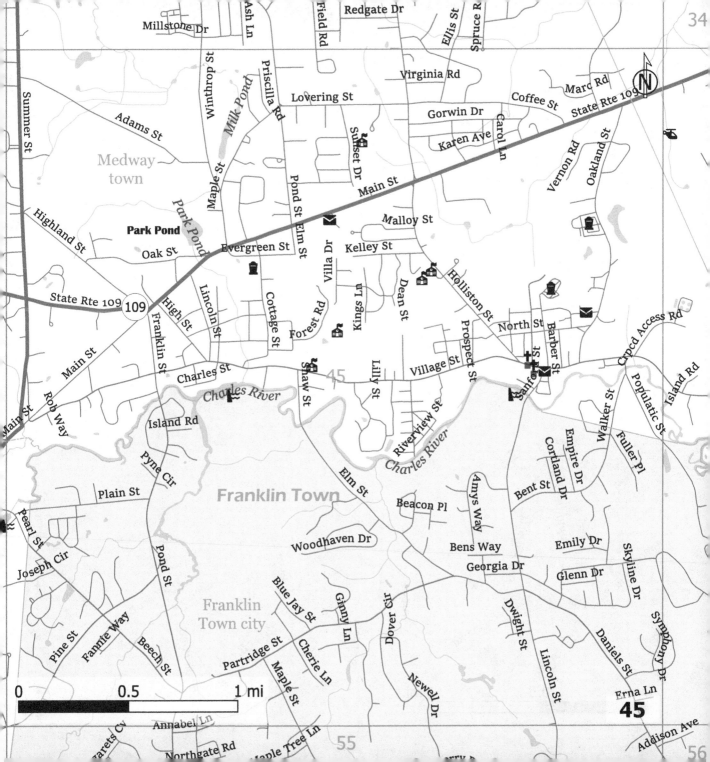

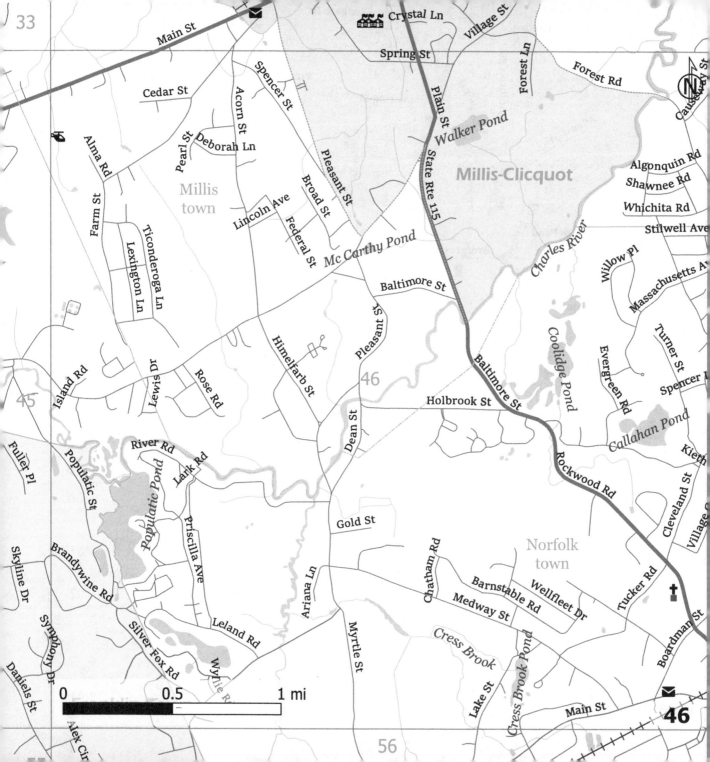

Main St

Cedar St

Spencer St

Crystal Ln

Village St

Spring St

Forest Ln

Forest Rd

Acorn St

Pearl St

Deborah Ln

Alma Rd

Plain St

Walker Pond

Millis-Clicquot

Algonquin Rd

Shawnee Rd

Whichita Rd

Farm St

Millis
town

Pleasant St

State Rte 115

Stilwell Ave

Lincoln Ave

Broad St

Federal St

Mc Carthy Pond

Charles River

Willow Pl

Massachusetts Av

Ticonderoga Ln

Lexington Ln

Baltimore St

Coolidge Pond

Turner St

Spencer St

Himelfarb St

Pleasant St

46

Evergreen Rd

Island Rd

Lewis Dr

Rose Rd

Holbrook St

Baltimore St

Callahan Pond

Kieth

Fuller Pl

River Rd

Lark Rd

Dean St

Rockwood Rd

Cleveland St

Village

Populatic St

Populatic Pond

Priscilla Ave

Gold St

Norfolk
town

Tucker Rd

Skyline Dr

Brandywine Rd

Ariana Ln

Chatham Rd

Barnstable Rd

Wellfleet Dr

Boardman St

Symphony Dr

Silver Fox Rd

Leland Rd

Myrtle St

Medway St

Cress Brook

Lake St

Cress Brook Pond

Daniels St

Wylie R

0   0.5   1 mi

Main St

Alex Cir

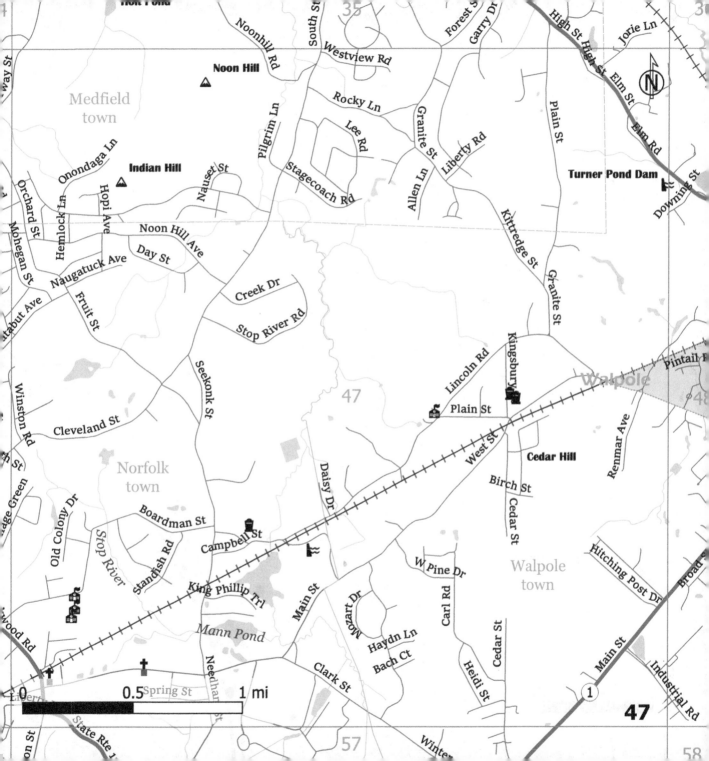

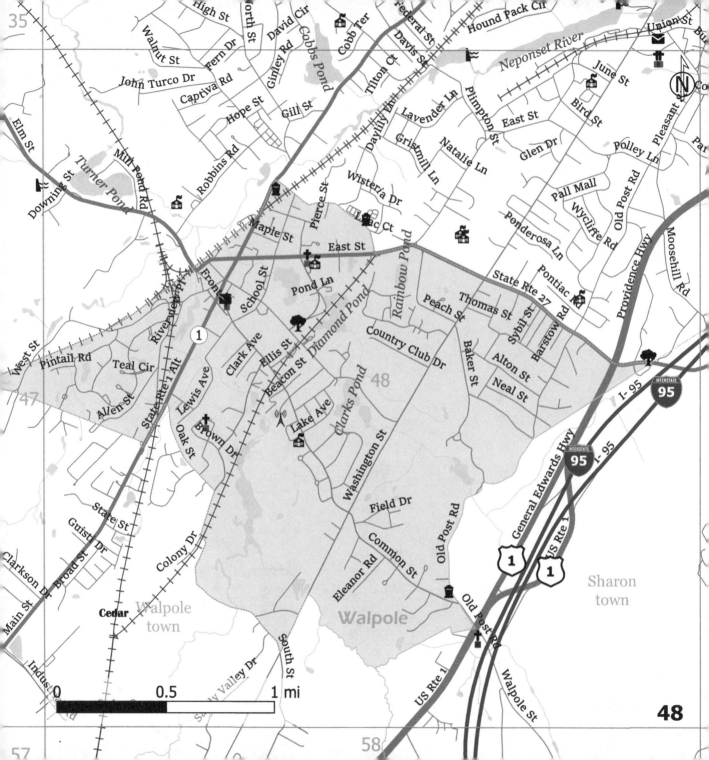

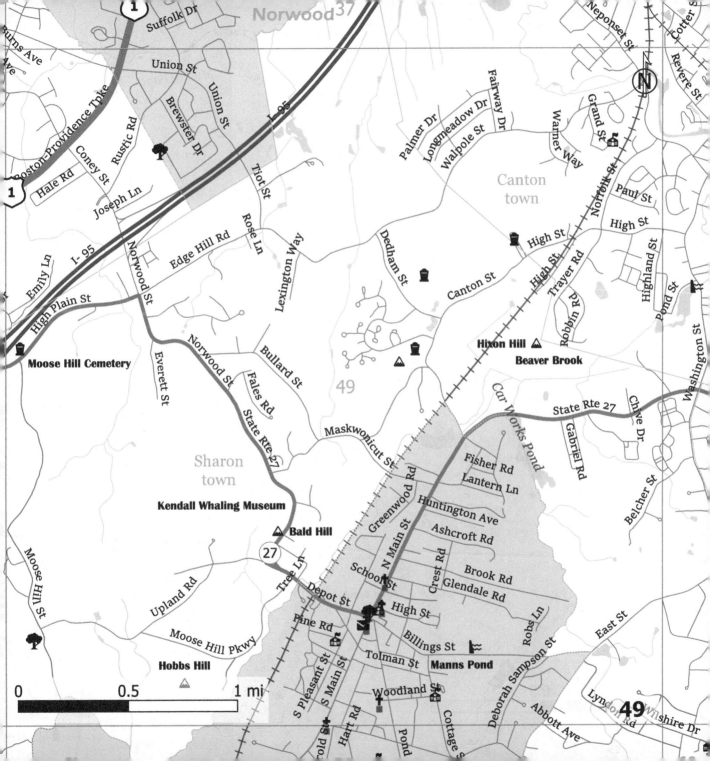

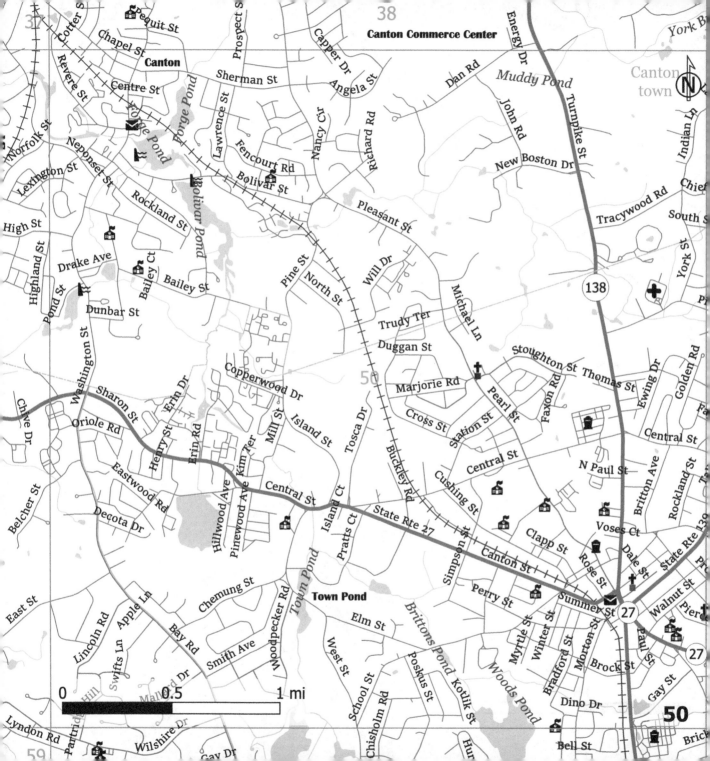

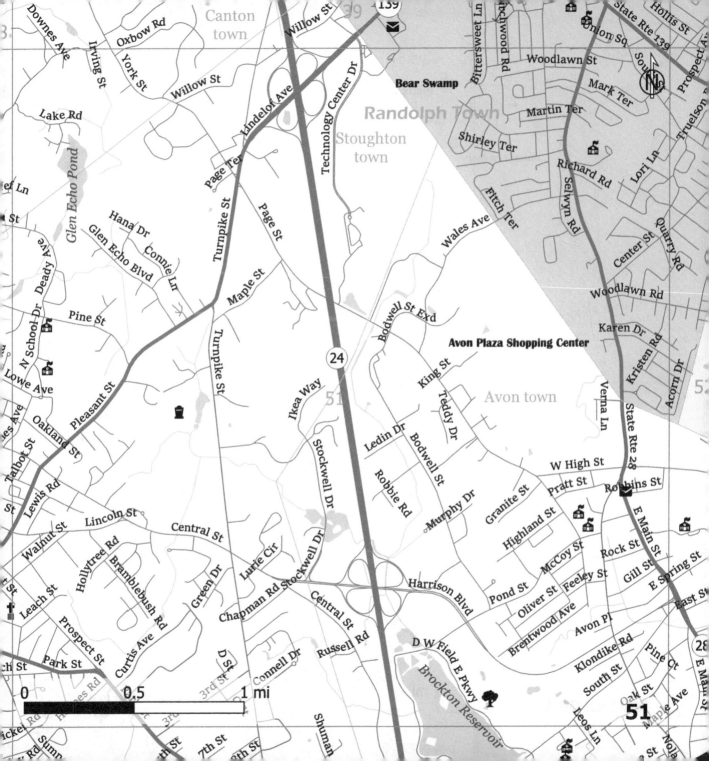

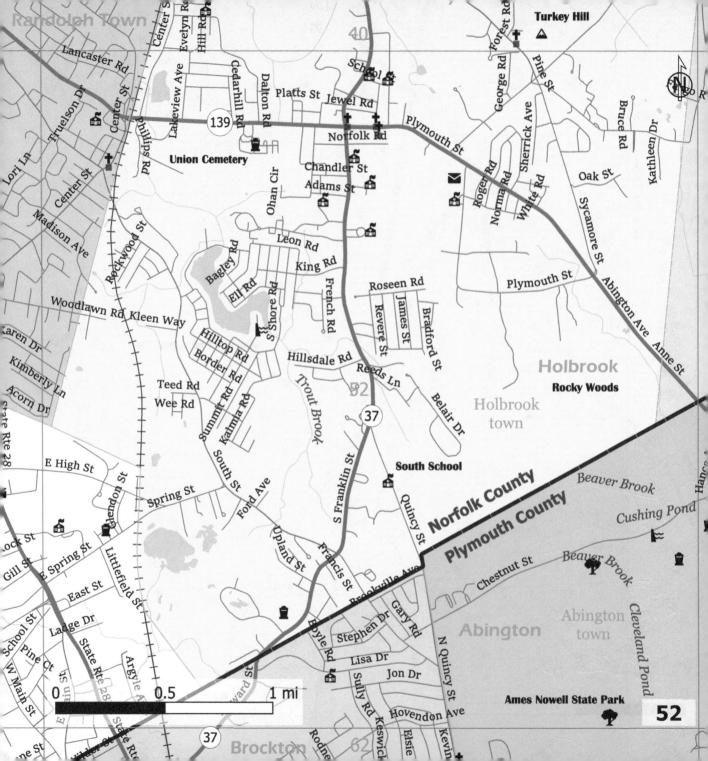

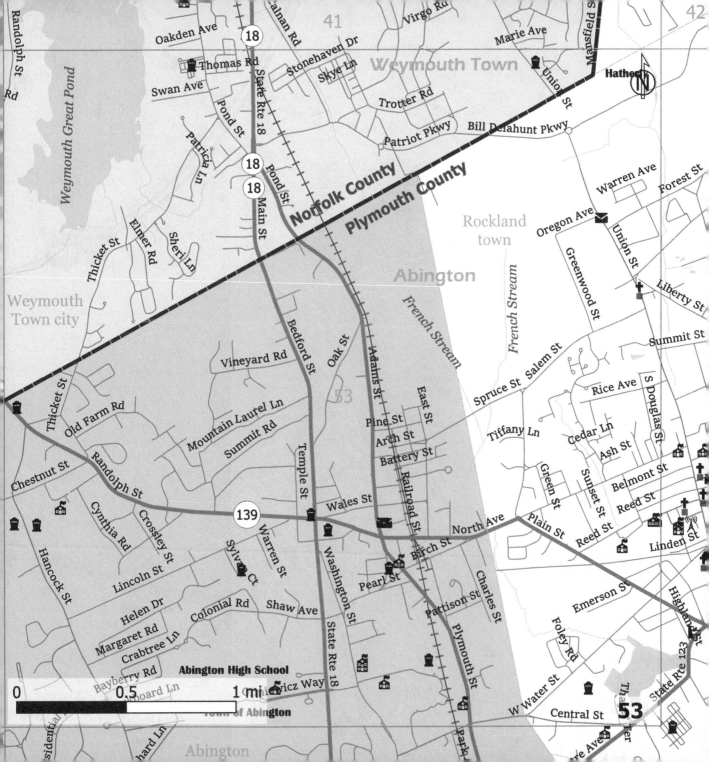

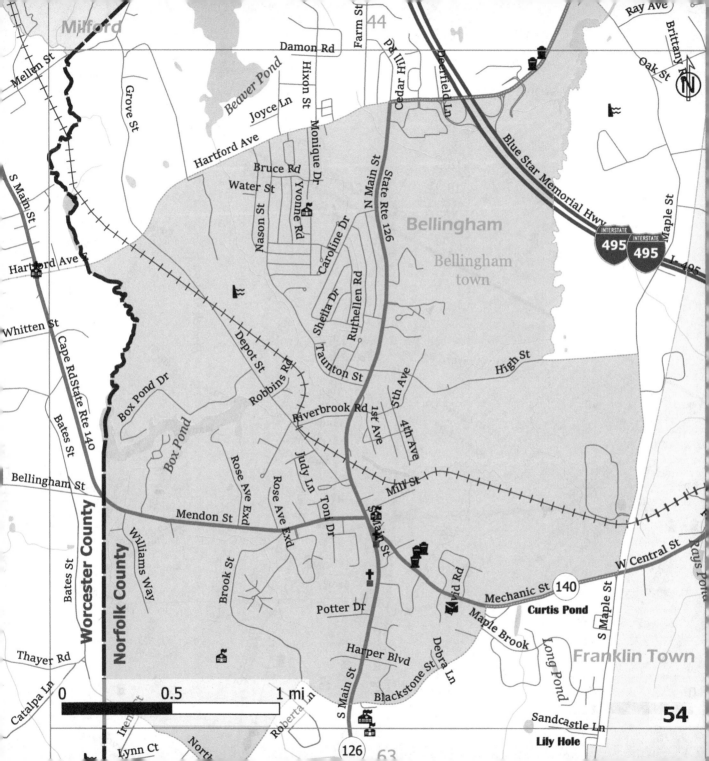

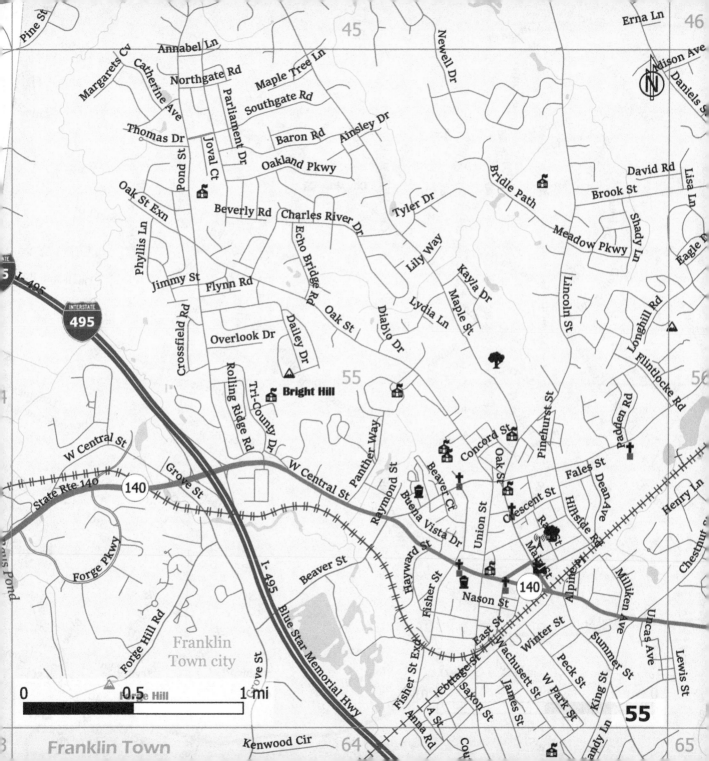

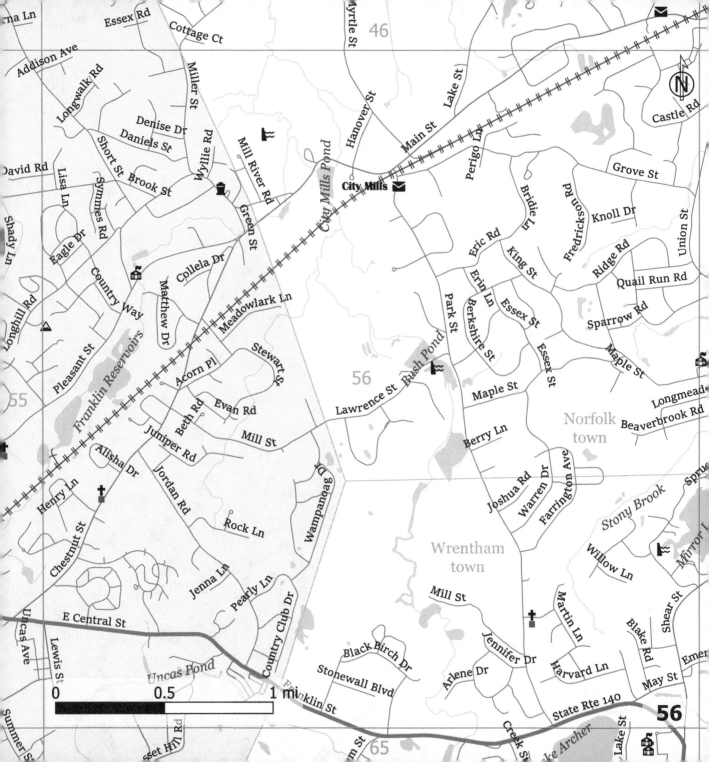

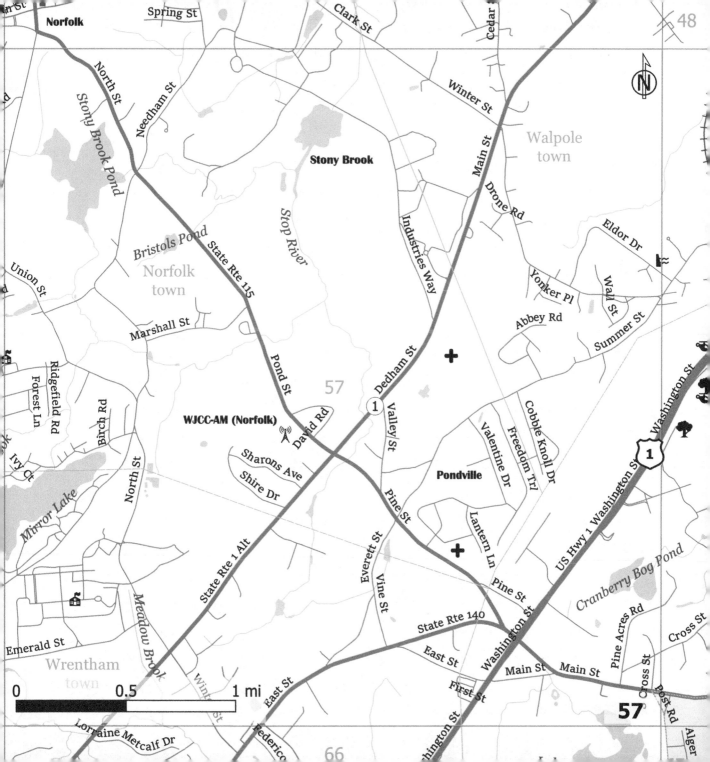

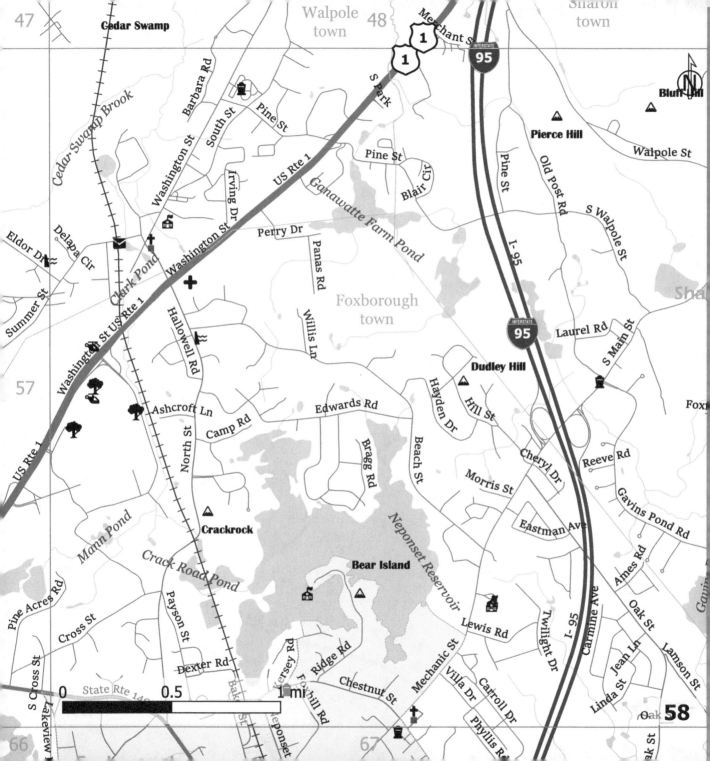

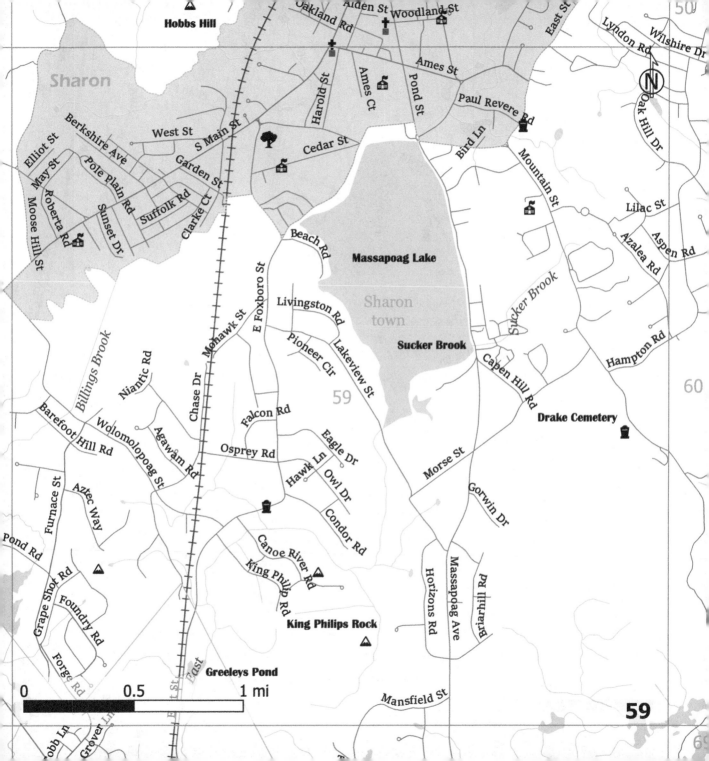

Hobbs Hill

Sharon

Aiden St Woodland St

Oakland Rd

East St

Lyndon Rd

Wilshire Dr

Oak Hill Dr

Ames St

N

Harold St

Ames Ct

Pond St

Paul Revere Rd

West St S Main St

Berkshire Ave

Elliot St

May St

Pole Plain Rd

Garden St

Cedar St

Bird Ln

Lilac St

Roberta Rd

Suffolk Rd

Sunset Dr

Clarke Ct

Mountain St

Azalea Rd

Aspen Rd

Moose Hill St

Beach Rd

Massapoag Lake

Sucker Brook

Billings Brook

Mohawk St

E Foxboro St

Livingston Rd

Sharon
town

Niantic Rd

Chase Dr

Pioneer Cir

Lakeview St

Sucker Brook

Capen Hill Rd

Hampton Rd

60

Barefoot Hill Rd

Wolomolopoag St

Agawam Rd

Falcon Rd

Drake Cemetery

Osprey Rd

Eagle Dr

59

Pond Rd

Furnace St

Aztec Way

Hawk Ln

Owl Dr

Morse St

Gorwin Rd

Grape Shot Rd

Foundry Rd

Condor Rd

King Philip Rd

Canoe River Rd

Horizons Rd

Massapoag Ave

Briarhill Rd

Forge Rd

King Philips Rock

East St

0   0.5   1 mi

Greeleys Pond

Mansfield St

Hobb Ln

Grover Ln

59

60

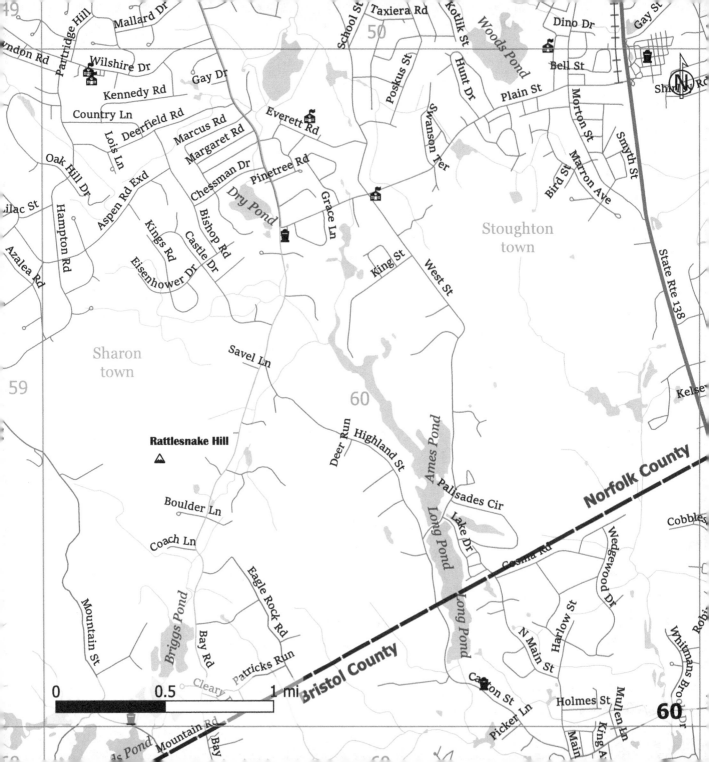

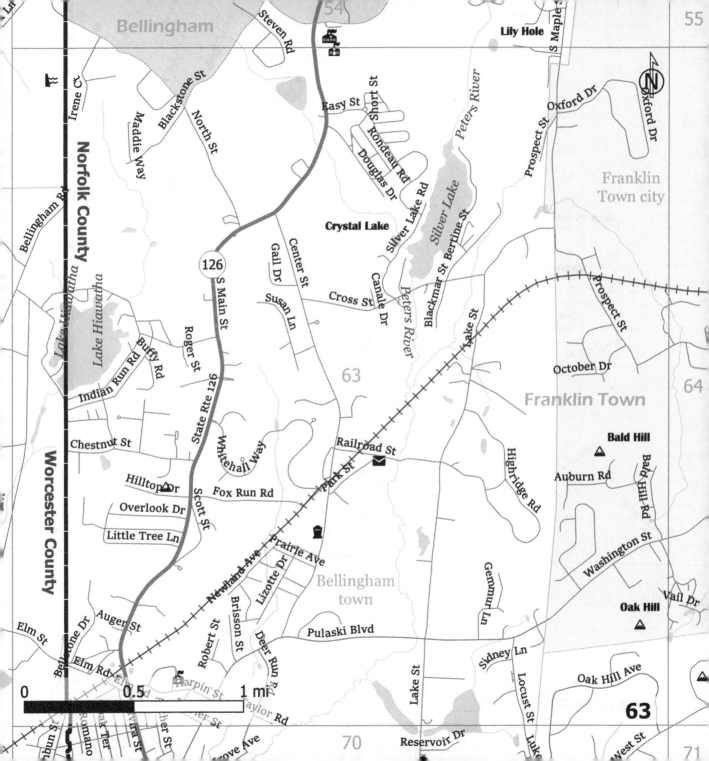

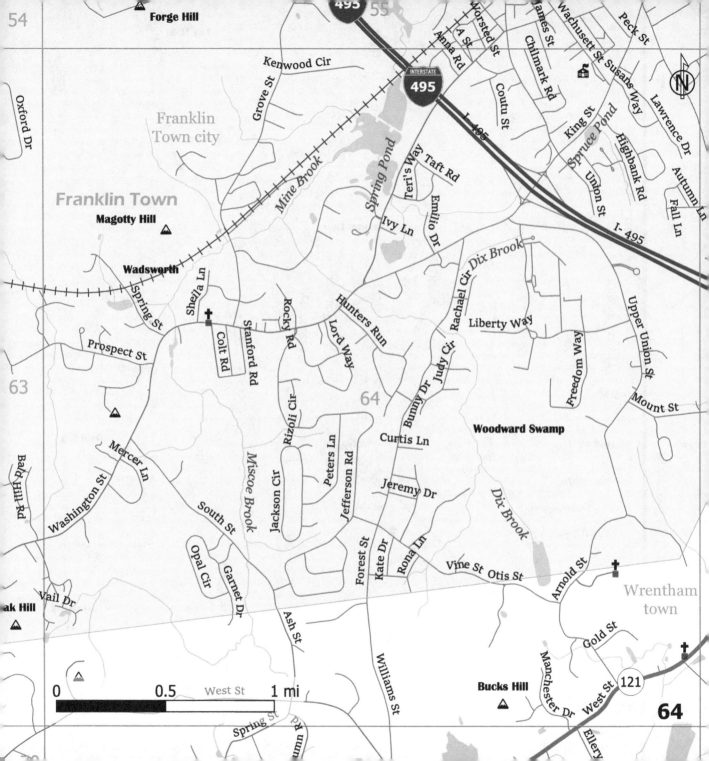

Forge Hill

54

55

Oxford Dr

Kenwood Cir

Grove St

Franklin
Town city

Mine Brook

Franklin Town

Magotty Hill

Wadsworth

Spring St

Sheila Ln

Colt Rd

Prospect St

Stanford Rd

Rocky Rd

Rizoli Cir

Jackson Cir

Miscoe Brook

Peters Ln

Jefferson Rd

63

64

Mercer Ln

Washington St

Badd Hill Rd

South St

Opal Cir

Garnet Dr

ak Hill

Vail Dr

Ash St

Williams St

West St

Spring St

INTERSTATE 495

INTERSTATE 495

Worsted St

A St

Anna Rd

Coutu St

James St

Chilmark Rd

Wachusett St Susans Way

King St

Spruce Pond

Highbank Rd

Union St

I-495

Peck St

Lawrence Dr

Autumn Ln

Fall Ln

Spring Pond

Teri's Way

Taft Rd

Ivy Ln

Emilio Dr

Rachael Cir Dix Brook

Liberty Way

Upper Union St

Freedom Way

Mount St

Hunters Run

Lord Way

Bunny Dr

Judy Cir

Curtis Ln

Woodward Swamp

Jeremy Dr

Dix Brook

Forest St

Kate Dr

Rona Ln

Vine St Otis St

Arnold St

Wrentham
town

Gold St

Manchester Dr

West St

121

64

Bucks Hill

Ellery

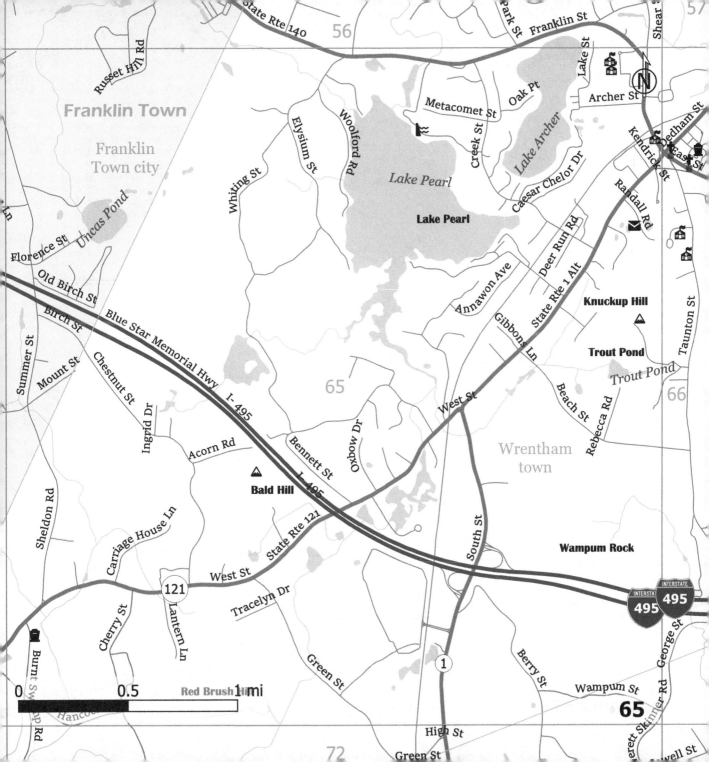

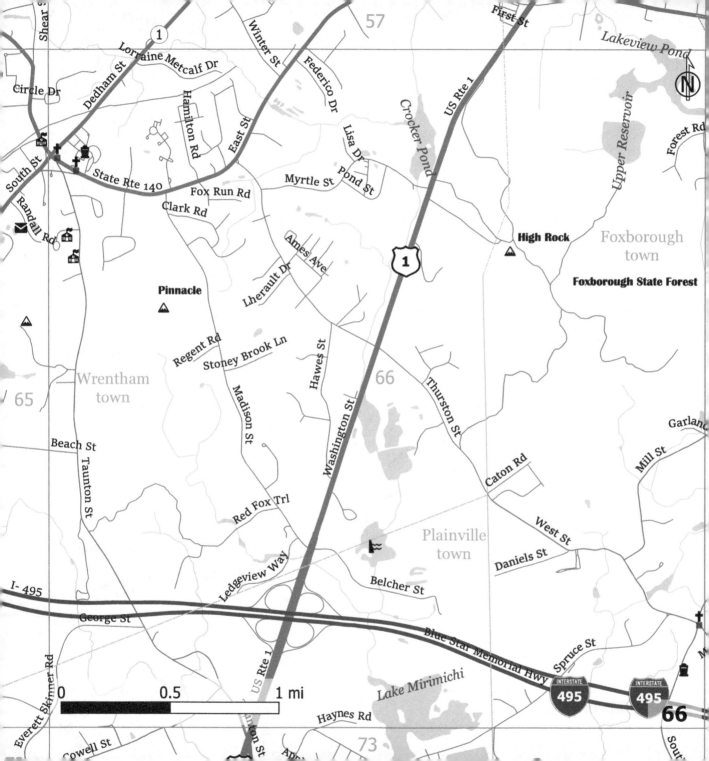

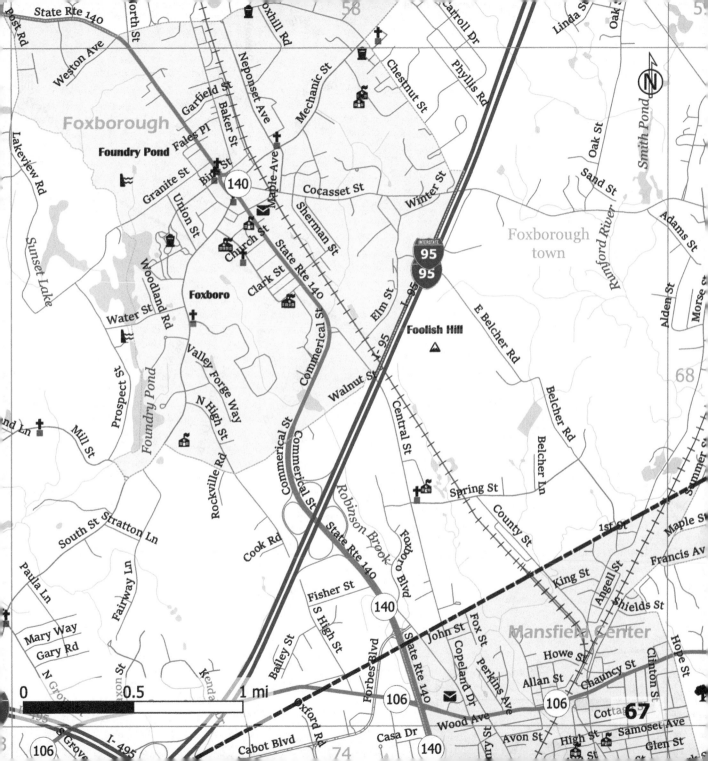

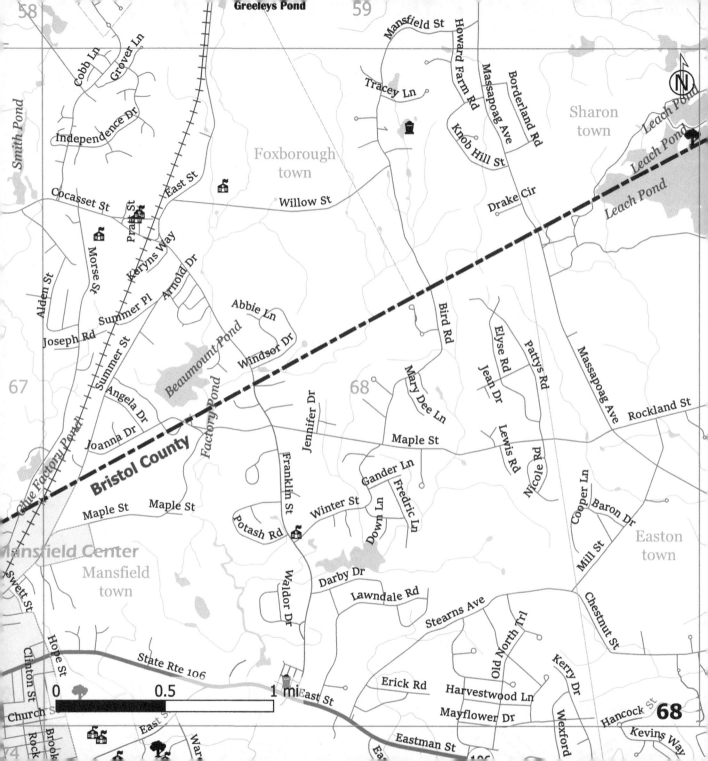

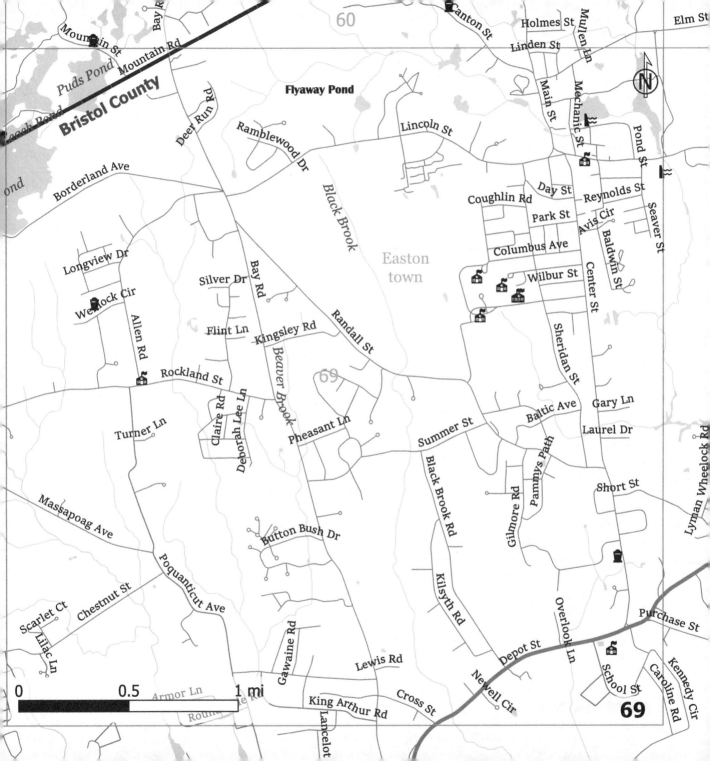

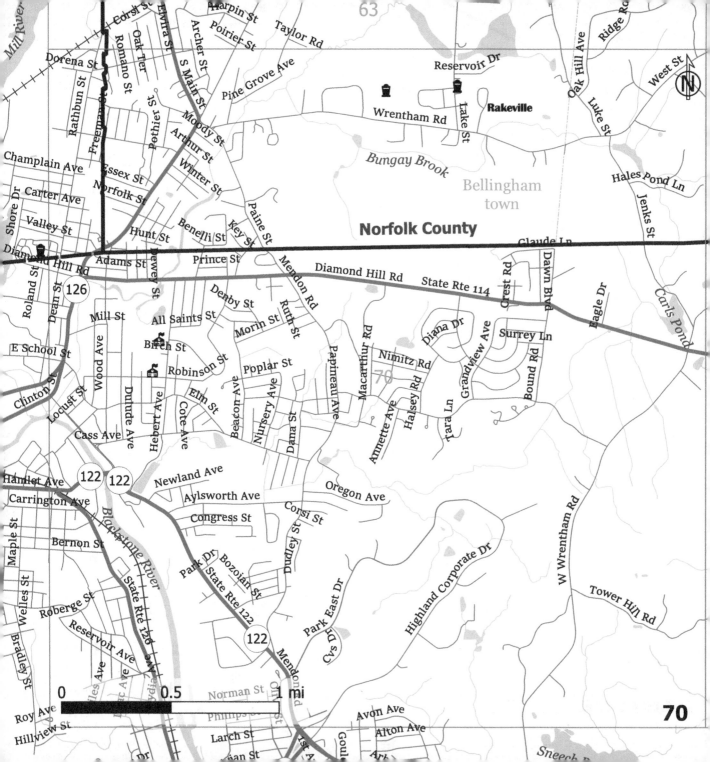

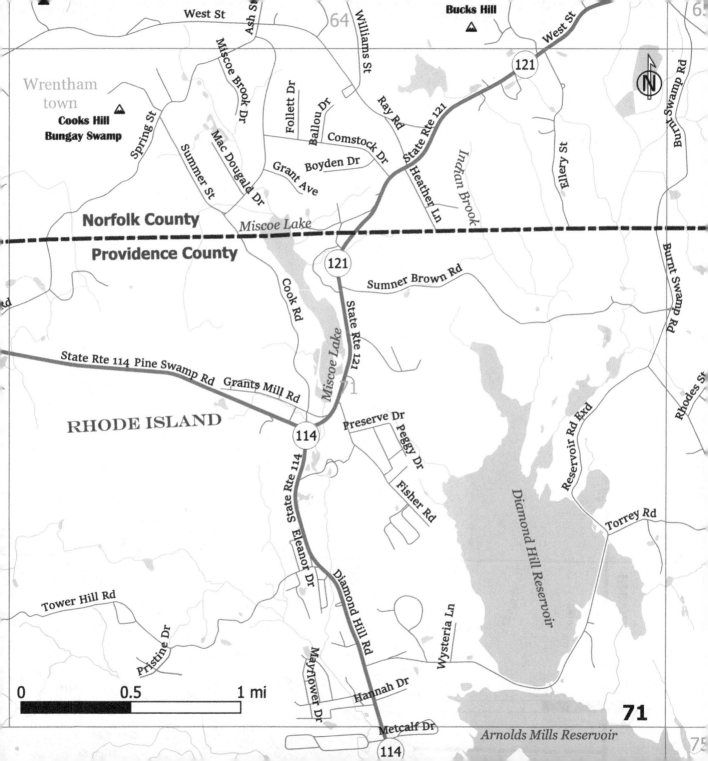

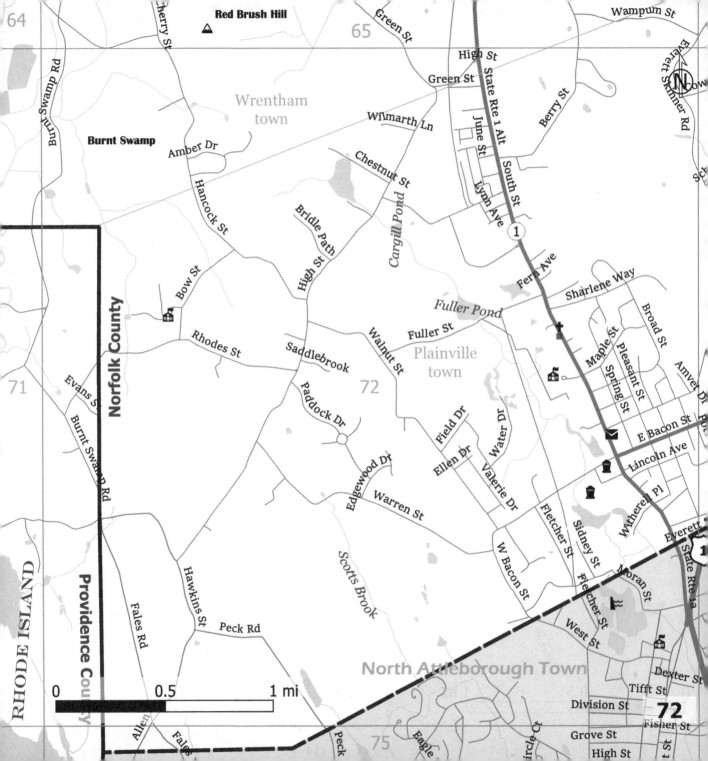

64

Red Brush Hill

65

Wampum St

Green St

High St

Green St

Berry St

Everett Skinner Rd

N

Wrentham
town

Wilmarth Ln

June St

Lynn Ave

State Rte 1 Alt

South St

Burnt Swamp

Amber Dr

Chestnut St

Cargill Pond

1

Fern Ave

Sharlene Way

Hancock St

Bridle Path

Fuller Pond

Broad St

Maple St

Bow St

High St

Fuller St

Pleasant St

Spring St

Rhodes St

Saddlebrook

Walnut St

Plainville
town

E Bacon St

Amvet Dr

Norfolk County

71

Evans St

Burnt Swamp Rd

72

Paddock Dr

Field Dr

Water Dr

Lincoln Ave

Witherell Pl

Ellen Dr

Valerie Dr

Edgewood Dr

Warren St

Everett

State Rte 1a

Fletcher St

Sidney St

Moran St

Scotts Brook

W Bacon St

1

Hawkins St

Fales Rd

Peck Rd

West St

Fletcher St

Dexter St

RHODE ISLAND

Providence County

0   0.5   1 mi

North Attleborough Town

Tifft St

Division St

72

Fisher St

Allen

Fales

Peck

75

Eagle

Circle Ct

Grove St

High St

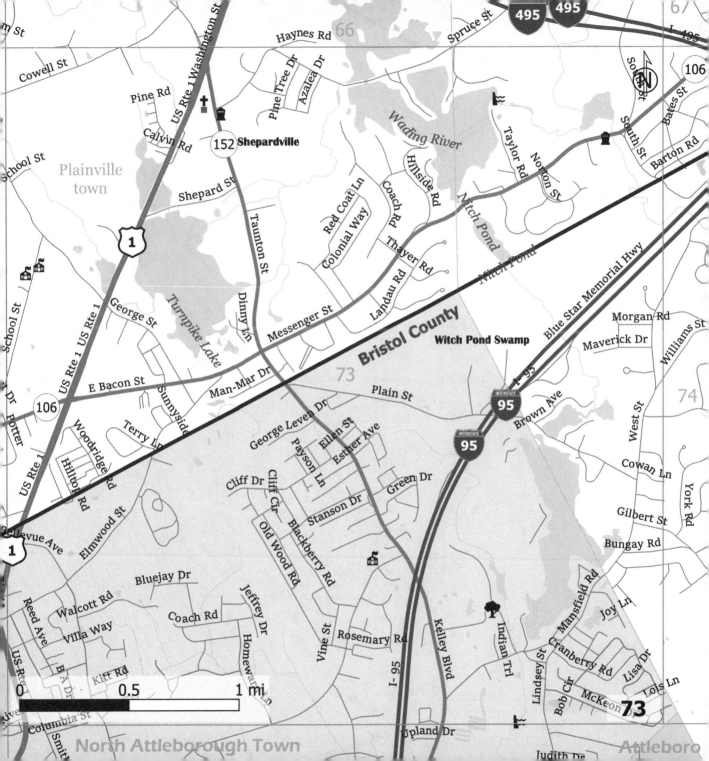

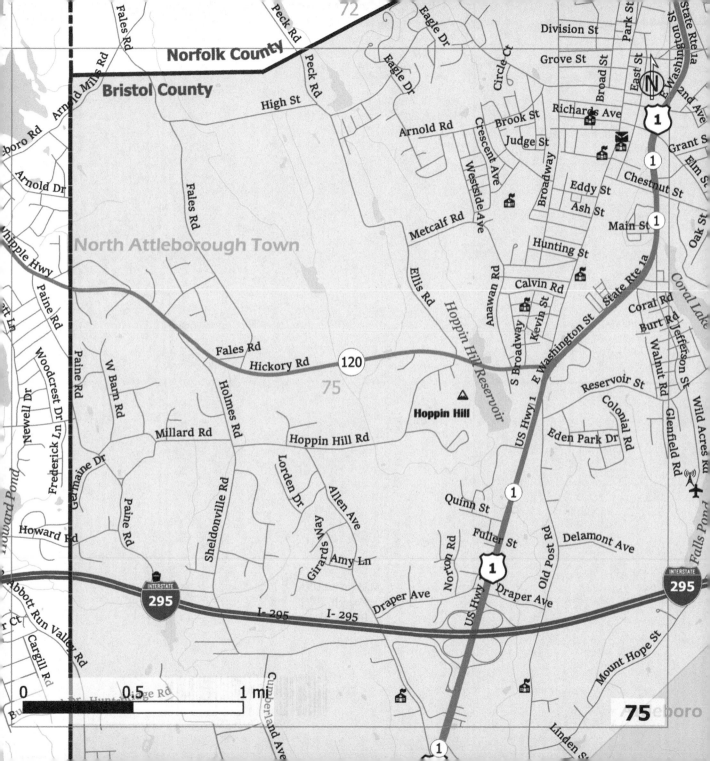

Made in the USA
Coppell, TX
10 July 2023

18958061R00044